Communications in Computer and Information Science   760

Commenced Publication in 2007
Founding and Former Series Editors:
Alfredo Cuzzocrea, Xiaoyong Du, Orhun Kara, Ting Liu, Dominik Ślęzak,
and Xiaokang Yang

More information about this series at http://www.springer.com/series/7899

Dimitris Kotzinos · Dominique Laurent
Jean-Marc Petit · Nicolas Spyratos
Yuzuru Tanaka (Eds.)

Information Search, Integration, and Personlization

11th International Workshop, ISIP 2016
Lyon, France, November 1–4, 2016
Revised Selected Papers

 Springer

Editors
Dimitris Kotzinos
Saint Lab ETIS
Université de Cergy-Pontoise
Pontoise
France

Dominique Laurent
Laboratoire ETIS
Université de Cergy Pontoise
Cergy Pontoise
France

Jean-Marc Petit
Dept Informatique INSA Lyon
Université de Lyon
Villeurbanne Cedex
France

Nicolas Spyratos
LRI
University of Paris
Orsay
France

Yuzuru Tanaka
Graduate School of Information Science
    Knowledge Media Laboratory
Hokkaido University
Sapporo
Japan

ISSN 1865-0929   ISSN 1865-0937   (electronic)
Communications in Computer and Information Science
ISBN 978-3-319-68281-5   ISBN 978-3-319-68282-2   (eBook)
DOI 10.1007/978-3-319-68282-2

Library of Congress Control Number: 2017954911

Printed on acid-free paper

This Springer imprint is published by Springer Nature
The registered company is Springer International Publishing AG
The registered company address is: Gewerbestrasse 11, 6330 Cham, Switzerland

Preface

This book contains the selected research papers presented at ISIP 2016, the 11th International Workshop on Information Search, Integration and Personalization. After being organized in France, Japan, Thailand, Malaysia, and USA (North Dakota), this year the workshop was held again in France, reflecting the goal of alternating places while widening the audience. More precisely, the workshop took place in 2016 at the University Claude Bernard Lyon 1, November 3–4.

Two keynote speeches (whose abstracts are included here) were given during the workshop:

- Professor Jun Adachi (National Institute of Informatics, Japan), *"Social CPS: Its Concept and Practical Experience Acquired in the Demonstrative Experiment"*
- Professor Paolo Papotti (Arizona State University, USA), *"Detecting Data Errors: Where Are We and What Needs to Be Done?"*

There were 30 presentations of scientific papers, of which 13 were submitted to the post-workshop peer review. The international Program Committee selected eight papers to be included in the proceedings.

The themes of the presented and/or submitted papers reflected today's diversity of research topics as well as the rapid development of interdisciplinary research. With increasingly sophisticated research in science and technology, there is a growing need for interdisciplinary and international availability, distribution, and exchange of the latest research results, in organic forms, including not only research papers and multimedia documents, but also various tools developed for measurement, analysis, inference, design, planning, simulation, and production as well as the related large data sets. Similar needs are also growing for the interdisciplinary and international availability, distribution, and exchange of ideas and works among artists, musicians, designers, architects, directors, and producers. These contents, including multimedia documents, application tools, and services are being accumulated on the Web, as well as in local and global databases, at a remarkable speed that we have never experienced with other kinds of publishing media. Large amounts of content are now already on the Web, waiting for their advanced personal and/or public reuse. We need new theories and technologies for the advanced information search, integration through interoperation, and personalization of Web content as well as database content.

The ISIP 2016 workshop was organized to offer a forum for presenting original work and stimulating discussions and exchanges of ideas around these themes, focusing on the following topics.

- Data Quality
- Social Cyber-Physical Systems
- Information search in large data sets (databases, digital libraries, data warehouses)
- Comparison of different information search technologies, approaches, and algorithms

- Novel approaches to information search
- Personalized information retrieval and personalized Web search
- Data Analytics (Data Mining, Data Warehousing)
- Integration of Web services, Knowledge bases, Digital libraries
- Federation of Smart Objects

ISIP started as a series of Franco-Japanese workshops in 2003, and its first edition took place under the auspices of the French embassy in Tokyo, which provided the financial support along with JSPS (Japanese Society for the Promotion of Science). Up until 2012, the workshops alternated between Japan and France, and attracted increasing interest from both countries. Then, motivated by the success of the first editions of the workshop, participants from countries other than France or Japan volunteered to organize it in their home country.

The history of past ISIP workshops is as follows:

- 2003: First ISIP in Sapporo (June 30 to July 2, Meme Media Lab, Hokkaido University, Japan)
- 2005: Second ISIP in Lyon (May 9–11, University Claude Bernard Lyon 1, France)
- 2007: Third ISIP in Sapporo (June 27–30, Meme Media Laboratory, Hokkaido University, Japan)
- 2008: 4th ISIP in Paris (October 6–8, Tour Montparnasse, Paris, France)
- 2009: 5th ISIP in Sapporo (July 6–8, Meme Media Laboratory, Hokkaido University, Japan)
- 2010: 6th ISIP in Lyon (October 11–13, University Claude Bernard Lyon 1, France)
- 2012: 7th ISIP in Sapporo (October 11–13, Meme Media Laboratory, Hokkaido University, Japan)
- 2013: 8th ISIP in Bangkok (September 16–18, Centara Grand and Bangkok Convention Centre Central World Bangkok, Thailand).
- 2014: 9th ISIP in Kuala Lumpur (October 9–10, HELP University, Kuala Lumpur, Malaysia).
- 2015: 10th ISIP in Grand Forks (October 1–2, University of North Dakota, Grand Forks, North Dakota, USA)

Originally, the workshops were intended for a Franco-Japanese audience, with the occasional invitation of researchers from other countries as keynote speakers. The proceedings of each workshop were published informally, as a technical report of the hosting institution. One exception was the 2005 workshop, selected papers of which were published by the *Journal of Intelligent Information Systems* in its special issue for ISIP 2005 (Vol. 31, Number 2, October 2008). The original goal of the ISIP workshop series was to create close synergies between a selected group of researchers from the two countries; and indeed, several collaborations, joint publications, joint student supervisions, and research projects originated from participants of the workshop.

After the first six workshops, the organizers concluded that the workshop series had reached a mature state with an increasing number of researchers participating every year. As a result, the organizers decided to open up the workshop to a larger audience by inviting speakers from over ten countries at ISIP 2012, ISIP 2013, ISIP 2014, as well as at ISIP 2015. The effort to attract an even larger international audience led to the workshop being organized in countries other than France and Japan. This will continue in the years to come. During the past four years in particular, an extensive effort was made to include in the Program Committee academics coming from around the globe, giving the workshop an even more international character and disseminating its information and results globally. We expect this to have an important effect in the participation of the workshop in the years to come.

The selected papers contained in this book are grouped into three major topics, namely, "Exploratory Analytics", "Mobility and Location Data Analytics", and "Large Graph Management"; they span major topics in information management research both modern and traditional.

We would like to express our appreciation to all the staff members of the organizing institution for the help, kindness, and support before during and after the workshop. Of course we also would like to cordially thank all speakers and participants of ISIP 2016 for their intensive discussions and exchange of new ideas. This book is an outcome of those discussions and exchanged ideas. Our thanks also go to the Program Committee members whose work was undoubtedly essential for the selection of the papers contained in this book.

July 2017
Jean-Marc Petit
Nicolas Spyratos
Yuzuru Tanaka

Abstracts of Keynote Speeches

Social CPS: Its Concept and Practical Experience Acquired in the Demonstrative Experiment

Jun Adachi

National Institute of Informatics, Japan

A cyber-physical system (CPS) is an IT-based system that grasps the physical world by sensing, then analyzes the acquired data in order to give feedback to the real world. This general scheme of CPS is expected to have diversified potential possibility to enhance the current systems, in particular complex and huge social systems that include interaction with humans. We call this "social CPS."

We have been conducting a research project titled "CPS-IIP: Integrated IT Platforms for Cyber-Physical Systems to Accelerate Implementation of Efficient Social Systems" since 2012, funded by the Japanese Ministry of Education, Culture, Sports, Science, and Technology.

In this talk, I will explain the concepts and the goals of the project, which includes implementation of two demonstrative systems as practical application of CPS to social systems: "Smart Snow Plowing" and "Human-Centric Energy Management." Our development of various basic technologies for CPS, such as data store and high-throughput processing systems, smart federated analytics with machine-learning techniques, and various sensing technologies for real-world data processing, will also be introduced.

Detecting Data Errors: Where Are We and What Needs to Be Done?

Paolo Papotti

Arizona State University, USA

Data cleaning has played a critical role in ensuring data quality for enterprise applications. Naturally, there has been extensive research in this area, and many data cleaning algorithms have been translated into tools to detect and to possibly repair certain classes of errors such as outliers, duplicates, missing values, and violations of integrity constraints. Since different types of errors may coexist in the same data set, we often need to run more than one kind of tool.

In a recent effort, we investigated two pragmatic questions: (1) are these tools robust enough to capture most errors in real-world data sets? and (2) what is the best strategy to holistically run multiple tools to optimize the detection effort? To answer these two questions, we obtained multiple data cleaning tools that utilize a variety of error detection techniques. We also collected five real-world data sets, for which we could obtain both the raw data and the ground truth on existing errors.

In this talk, we report our experimental findings on the errors detected by the tools we tested. First, we show that the coverage of each tool is well below 100%. Second, we show that the order in which multiple tools are run makes a big difference. Hence, we propose a holistic multi-tool strategy that orders the invocations of the available tools to maximize their benefit, while minimizing human effort in verifying results. Third, since this holistic approach still does not lead to acceptable error coverage, we discuss two simple strategies that have the potential to improve the situation, namely domain specific tools and data enrichment. We close this talk by reasoning about the errors that are not detectable by any of the tools we tested and possible directions of future research.

Organization

ISIP 2016 was organized by the University Claude Bernard Lyon 1, Lyon, France

Executive Committee

Co-chairs
Jean-Marc Petit — INSA de Lyon, France
Nicolas Spyratos — Paris-Sud University, France
Yuzuru Tanaka — Hokkaido University, Japan

Program Committee Chairs
Dimitris Kotzinos — University of Cergy-Pontoise, France
Dominique Laurent — University of Cergy-Pontoise, France

Local Organization
Sylvie Calabretto — INSA de Lyon, France
Fabien De Marchi — University Claude Bernard Lyon 1, France
Lea Laporte — INSA de Lyon, France
Jean-Marc Petit — INSA de Lyon, France
Pierre-Edouard Portier — INSA de Lyon, France
Mohand Said-Hacid — University Claude Bernard Lyon 1, France
Vasile-Marian Scuturici — INSA de Lyon, France
Romuald Thion — University Claude Bernard Lyon 1, France

Publicity Chair
Jean-Marc Petit — INSA de Lyon, France

Program Committee

Adaricheva, Kira — Hofstra University, Japan
Akaishi, Mina — Hosei University, Japan
Berti-Equille, Laure — Qatar Computing Research Institute, Qatar
Bonifati, Angela — University Claude Bernard Lyon 1, France
Bressan, Stephane — National University of Singapore, Singapore
Giacometti, Arnaud — Université François Rabelais de Tours, France
Grant, Emanuel S. — University of North Dakota, USA
Goebel, Randy — University of Alberta, Canada
Halfeld Ferrari Alves, Mirian — University of Orléans, France

Jen, Tao-Yuan — University of Cergy-Pontoise, France
Koudylakis, Haridimos — FORTH Institute of Computer Science, Greece
Kotzinos, Dimitris — University of Cergy-Pontoise, France

Contents

Exploratory Analytics

Towards User-Aware Rule Discovery

Venkata Vamsikrishna Meduri and Paolo Papotti[✉]

Arizona State University, Tempe, USA
{vmeduri,ppapotti}@asu.edu

Abstract. Rule discovery is a challenging but inevitable process in several data centric applications. The main challenges arise from the huge search space that needs to be explored, and from the noise in the data, which makes the mining results hardly useful. While existing state-of-the-art systems pose the users at the beginning and the end of the mining process, we argue that this paradigm must be revised and new rule mining algorithms should be developed to let the domain experts interact during the discovery process. We discuss how new systems that embrace this approach overcome current limitations and ultimately result in shorter time and smaller user effort for rule discovery.

1 Introduction

Rule discovery from data is of utmost importance given the applicability of rules in several real world data-centric applications such as cleaning [13,25,32], fraud detection [4,5], cybersecurity [22,28], smart cities [15,20], and database design [19,21,34]. While for many of these applications machine learning (ML) approaches have been designed, rules are still extremely popular in the industry [32]. In fact, rules are a favored choice to encode the background knowledge of the domain experts and ultimately take decisions over data. For example, financial services corporations manually create corpora of thousands of rules to identify fraudulent credit card transactions [24]. The main advantages of rule based approaches include the ability to work without training data, the possibility to debug them by non-experts, the potential to handle specialized infrequent patterns, and the semantically explainable and interpretable output [32].

In this work we focus on rules for data quality. We are interested in rules that go beyond traditional association rules [3], both in terms of complexity of the rule language and in terms of supported data models. Consider a scenario with credit card transactions by a customer, as shown in Fig. 1. A domain expert states that if there are two transactions from the same card and the same merchant, the transaction IDs must be consistent with the timestamps, or the transactions should be manually reviewed. In other words, if a transaction has a higher id than another one that is registered later, there must be a problem.

In this example, the rule is triggered because record T_2 for transaction with ID "XX216" is registered before transaction "XX214" in T_1. The rule can be formally stated by using the formalization of *Denial Constraints* (DCs) [10] as

© Springer International Publishing AG 2017
D. Kotzinos et al. (Eds.): ISIP 2016, CCIS 760, pp. 3–17, 2017.
DOI: 10.1007/978-3-319-68282-2_1

$$\forall T_\alpha, T_\beta \in R, \neg(T_\alpha.Merchant = T_\beta.Merchant \wedge T_\alpha.CreditCard =$$
$$T_\beta.CreditCard \wedge T_\alpha.TransID > T_\beta.TransID \wedge T_\alpha.Time < T_\beta.Time)$$

where the universal variable T_α and T_β over the records are used to define predicates that, if true at the same time, trigger the rule.

	TransID	ItemId	Merchant	CreditCard	Time
T_1	XX214	17683	PayPal	XXX7038	10:35:02
T_2	XX216	43266	PayPal	XXX7038	10:34:43

Fig. 1. Credit card transactions.

However, discovering rules is a difficult exercise. Current approaches for rule discovery treat the algorithm as a black box, where the users are only engaged in the definition of the input parameters, such as the minimum support to consider a rule valid, and in the evaluation of the ultimate output. Unfortunately, these design choices make such approaches hard to use in real-world scenarios for three main reasons.

1. In the input definition step, several parameters strongly impact the final output, but are very hard to set upfront. Examples of such parameters include the percentage of tolerance to noise to discover approximate rules, or the way to select constants to be considered for rule discovery. These parameters are rarely known apriori, but tuning them with a trial-and-error approach is infeasible, given the large number of possible value combinations and the long running execution times for the mining, as discussed next.
2. Complexity in the mining of the rules comes from both the size of the schema and the size of the data. The schema complexity is exponential in the number of attributes, as all combinations of attributes must be tested [10]. For example, for the transactions example presented in Fig. 1, the rule may also need to involve attribute ItemId. Moreover, if the language supports complex pairwise rules, such as denial constraints or de-duplication rules, the complexity is quadratic over the number of tuples.
3. In the output consumption, the number of rules that hold over the data is usually large, especially when constants and approximate rules are allowed, as they are often needed in practice. Moreover, when tolerance to noise in the data is required, semantically valid rules are mixed with incorrect rules because of dirty values in the data. This problem is alleviated by pruning mechanisms and ranking, but ultimately it leads to a large amount of time spent by the domain experts to identify the valid rules among the thousands that hold on the data.

In addition to these shortcomings, we should consider the limits in terms of the expressive power in the existing solutions. Popular rules expressed with ETL or procedural languages employ *User Defined Functions* (UDFs) to specify special comparisons among values or complex look up functions. These specialized functions lead to more powerful rules, but the discovery of the right function is hard, as it is domain and dataset specific. Consider Temporal Functional Dependencies (TFDs), which are FDs that hold only during a certain time period, e.g., "the same person cannot be in two different places at the same time" [1,31]. Discovering the appropriate functions (the absolute time difference between timestamps) from a given library of UDFs [30,33] and the correct temporal values (the correct "same time" duration) is hard. These hard discovery cases lead to new input parameters, longer execution times, and larger number of output rules, thus exacerbating the three problems listed above.

We believe that the most promising way to overcome the limits of traditional approaches is to rethink discovering algorithms to make them *user-aware*. This change of perspective should cover all the aspects mentioned above: a more natural input for the users, incremental efficient algorithms to enable interactive response time, and a simpler and more effective way to identify the useful rules. As an orthogonal dimension, the new systems should also embrace a language that can use libraries of user-defined functions, in order to discover more powerful rules. In order to prune the huge unwanted search space while retaining high expressive power, we can use human support in the search algorithm as early as possible, so that it can steer the search in the right direction.

In the following, we first describe the main challenges in creating such new systems (Sect. 2), and we then discuss new approaches that we believe are heading in the correct direction (Sect. 3).

2   Why Rule Discovery Is Hard

In this Section, we first introduce formally a class of rules that will be used in the examples, and briefly give intuitions about other relevant classes. We then discuss rule discovery algorithms in general. Finally, we give the five main challenges in rule discovery.

2.1   Denial Constraints

Consider the example in Fig. 2 with items from a chain of grocery stores in three states, "AZ", "CA" and "WA". Assume that only "Shoes" from the store in state "AZ" and "EarPhones" from the store in "WA" are labeled as "General"; in any other state both items can only be listed under the type "FootWear" and "Electronics", respectively. The highlighted value for the Type indicates an error in tuple r_3, as the entry "EarPhones" has been labeled "General" instead of "Electronics" in "AZ".

For a relation R, we use a notation for DCs of the form
$$\varphi : \forall t_\alpha, t_\beta, t_\gamma, \ldots \in R, \neg(P_1 \wedge \ldots \wedge P_m)$$
where P_i is of the form $v_1 \phi v_2$ or $v_1 \phi c$ with $v_1, v_2 \in t_x.A, x \in \{\alpha, \beta, \gamma, \ldots\}, A \in R$, $\phi \in \{=, <, >, \neq, \leq, \geq\}$, and c is a constant.

Assume that a mining algorithm comes up with several approximate rules for the relation in Fig. 2. We use attribute abbreviations for readability.

	ItemID	Location	Title	Description	Type
r_1	17683	AZ	Levis	Shoes	General
r_2	34987	CA	AllStar	Shoes	FootWear
r_3	14325	AZ	Samsung	EarPhones	General
r_4	82971	WA	Nokia	EarPhones	General
r_5	9286	CA	Toshiba	EarPhones	Electronics

Fig. 2. Items in a chain of grocery stores.

$$R_1 : \forall T_\alpha \in R, \neg(T_\alpha.Desc. = \text{``}EarPhones\text{''} \wedge T_\alpha.Type \neq \text{``}Electronics\text{''})$$
$$R_2 : \forall T_\alpha \in R, \neg(T_\alpha.Loc. = \text{``}AZ\text{''} \wedge T_\alpha.Desc. = \text{``}EarPhones\text{''} \wedge$$
$$T_\alpha.Type \neq \text{``}Electronics\text{''})$$
$$R_3 : \forall T_\alpha \in R, \neg(T_\alpha.Desc. = \text{``}Shoes\text{''} \wedge T_\alpha.Type \neq \text{``}General\text{''})$$
$$R_4 : \forall T_\alpha \in R, \neg(T_\alpha.Loc. = \text{``}AZ\text{''} \wedge T_\alpha.Desc. = \text{``}Shoes\text{''} \wedge$$
$$T_\alpha.Type \neq \text{``}General\text{''})$$
$$R_5 : \forall T_\alpha, T_\beta \in R, \neg(T_\alpha.Desc. = T_\beta.Desc. \wedge T_\alpha.Type \neq T_\beta.Type)$$
$$R_6 : \forall T_\alpha, T_\beta \in R, \neg(T_\alpha.Loc. = T_\beta.Loc. \wedge T_\alpha.Desc. = T_\beta.Desc \wedge$$
$$T_\alpha.Type \neq T_\beta.Type)$$

Only some of the approximate rules that have been automatically discovered are correct. Rule R_1 states that all "EarPhones" should be binned into the type "Electronics", and identifies tuple r_4 as a violation while is not the case. Hence, R_1 is an incorrect rule. Rule R_2 is correct and identifies the error in r_3. However, it only enforces our domain knowledge for "EarPhones" and not for "Shoes". Since "Shoes" in "AZ" can be misclassified to any other type than "General", we need an additional rule, such as R_4, to detect all errors. Rule R_3 is correct for items sold in state "AZ", but would identify correct values as errors in the other states. Rule R_5 represents a functional dependency stating that the Description determines the Type and it is incorrect, since tuples r_4 and r_5 are erroneously identified as errors. Rule R_6 states that Location and Description determine the Type. This rule is correct and more general than the union of R_2 and R_4 as it does not depend on constants. In fact, it can enforce all the domain constraints on future tuples not restricted to just "Shoes" or "EarPhones".

2.2   Other Rule Types

Denial Constraints can express several common formalisms, such as Functional Dependencies [21,34] and Conditional Functional Dependencies [8,13]. They can express single tuple level rules (R_1–R_4) and table level rules, i.e., rules involving two or more tuples in the premise (R_5, R_6). Also they allow the use of variables and constants, and join across different relations. However, rule types are not limited to what we presented above. There are several other data quality rule types that are common in practice.

Regular-expression based rules specify constraints on textual patterns in a tuple [18] and lead to data transformations such as substring extraction, delimiter identification, and the specification of filters. For instance, a rule may state that only 5-digit numbers in the ItemID attribute of a tuple are allowed.

A very important problem where rules have proven their effectiveness is Entity Resolution [25,33]. The goal here is to perform de-duplication, i.e., to identify pairs and group of records that refer to the same real-world entity. An exemplary rule for the item data in Fig. 2 may state that two items should be merged if they have very similar ItemID and the same Location and Title.

Another example of rule types are inference rules, which suggest when two entities respect a particular relationship in a Knowledge Base [16]. These rules help infer and add missing knowledge to the KB. An inference rule can state that two persons sharing a child are married, therefore a new fact can be inferred in the KB. Inference rules are different from association rules [3], which do not derive new facts, but are popular in relational databases to discover interesting relations between variables, e.g., "If a client bought tomatoes and hamburgers, then she is likely to also buy buns".

Finally, lookup rules use an external reliable source of information which can be exploited up to identify errors in the database. The external source can either be a Knowledge Base (KB) [11] or a table of master data [14]. The discovery process tries to map the columns in the relation of interest to the external, reliable source. The resulting rule can then be used to verify if the relation conforms to the external source. For example, in Fig. 2, a rule would map the attributes Title and Type in the relation to two columns occurring in a master table, or to a $hasType(Title, Type)$ relationship in a KB. Every erroneous entry for Type, such as "Vegetables" for the Title "Levis", is identified as an error because it violates the mapping stated in the rule. A lookup rule for the example in Fig. 2 and a master table M can be expressed in a DC as follows.

$$R_7 : \forall T_\alpha \in R, T_\beta \in M \neg (T_\alpha.Title = T_\beta.ItemTitle \land T_\alpha.Type \neq T_\beta.Class)$$

The rule states that if the Title of a tuple in the relation is equal to an ItemTitle value in the master data, then the value in the relation for Type should match the corresponding value specified by Class in the master data, otherwise there must be an error in the relation.

2.3   Discovering Rules

All the different kinds of rules share challenges in their discovery process. We first give an intuition of how these mining algorithms work in general, and we then discuss their challenges in real-world applications. We divide the algorithms into two main categories.

Lattice traversal algorithms. The search space for rule discovery can be seen as a power set lattice of all attribute combinations. Several algorithms try to come up with the right way to traverse such a lattice. Different approaches have been tested, such as level-wise bottom-up traversal strategy and depth-first random walk. The commonality in these approaches is that they generate new rule candidates sequentially and immediately validate them individually (i.e., with a query over the data). The strategy to deal with the large search space is to prune it incrementally by inferring the validity of candidates that have not been checked yet. This test can be done exploiting the static analysis of the already discovered rules by using the minimality criterion, language axioms (e.g., augmentation and transitivity), and logical implication [17,19,21].

Difference- and agree-set algorithms. These algorithms model the search space in an alternative way by using difference and agree-sets. For pair-wise rules, the idea is to search for sets of attributes that agree on the values in the cross product of all tuples. Due to this change in the modelling, they do not try to successively check rules and aggressively prune the lattice search space. On the other hand, they look for attribute sets that agree on certain operators over the tuple values, since those can be in a dependency with other sets of attributes that also agree on some operator. Once obtained the agree-sets, the algorithms try derive the valid rules from them, either level-wise or by transforming them into a search tree that can traversed depth-first [10,34].

Rule discovery algorithms are then commonly extended in two directions.

First, in the discovery problem a rule is considered correct if there are no violations when applied over the data. However, in real-world scenarios, there are two main reasons to relax this requirement:

Overfitting. Data is dynamic and as more data becomes available, overfitting constraints on current data set can be problematic.

Errors. The common assumption is that errors constitute small percentage of data, thus discovering rules that hold for most of the dataset is a common approach to overcome this issue.

What is usually done is to modify the discovery statement into an *approximate rule discovery problem*. The goal is still to find valid rules, but now a rule is considered of interest if the percentage of violations (i.e., tuples not satisfying the rules) is below a given threshold. For this new problem, the original mining algorithm is revised to take this extension into account.

A second important and common aspect is the extension of the search space to also handle constants. The reason is that a given rule may not hold on the entire dataset, thus conditional rules are useful. Adding a new predicate with a constant is a straightforward operation, but the number of constant predicates is linear w.r.t. the number of constants in the active domain, which is usually very large. The common approach here is to focus on discovering rules for the frequent constants in the dataset [12,13].

As for the approximate version, the problem is revised to discover rules that involve constants with a frequency in the dataset above a given threshold. A common solution is to follow the "Apriori" approach to discover the frequent constants and then include only these constants in the predicates in the search space [10].

2.4   Challenges

We now use the example in Fig. 2 to illustrate the five main issues in rule discovery.

Scalability. Discovering rules is an expensive process. Consider rule discovery systems for Knowledge Bases [16]. A KB consists of <subject, relationship, object> triples such that a relationship holds over the <subject, object> pair. Since KBs do not have a generic schema presented upfront, the discovery of a rule is done by the enumeration of all the instances of <subject, object> pairs conforming to any of the relationships in the KB. In order to efficiently measure the support for the rules while discovering them, the entire KB is loaded into the main memory. Also, literals (constants) are removed from KB to make it fit the memory. Even with such extensive pre-pruning, these systems suffer from memory concerns and are hence constrained to mine rules with at most 3 atoms.

Traditional database rule mining methods suffer from similar limitations [8,13,21,26,34]. Since any subset of attributes can be part of a rule, there is an exponential number of rules to be tested w.r.t. the number of attributes in the input relation [10,19]. Also, rules that look over pairs of tuples with operators different from the equality, such as similarity comparisons for entity resolution [25,30] or not equal operators in DCs, have a quadratic complexity over the number of tuples in the dataset. Main memory algorithms can address this issue, but have obvious constraints on the maximum amount of data that can be handled.

Sampling seems a natural candidate to alleviate the memory concerns when generating rules. However, picking a representative sample that captures the subtleties of all the existing patterns in the data is not feasible. The main reason is the necessity to discover rules involving constants. For example, there is only a single tuple, r_1, in Fig. 2 for the fact that in "AZ", "Shoes" can be categorized as a "General" item. However, even if we sample three tuples r_2, r_3 and r_4 from the item list, thus with a larger sample size, we would not capture the specified pattern. The same issue applies with larger and more realistic datasets.

Another dimension in the complexity is the number of predicates that need to be tested. If we enable the use of a library of UDFs, each with its own configuration, such as a threshold for a similarity function in entity resolution [33], the search space becomes even larger and less tractable.

Noise. Noise is omnipresent in real datasets, and with percentages that can reach up to 26% of the data in applications such as data integration [1]. In addition, data can quickly turn stale. For instance, with concept drift, the composition of electronic goods like smartphones changes, thus there is a need of updating the classified category of their components [32]. In order to handle significant percentages of noise, rule discovery algorithms allow *approximate rules* that hold on most of the data. This is done by setting a threshold on the amount of admissible violations for a rule to be still considered valid. Approximate rules are learnt from the patterns in the data occurring with a percentage of exceptions below the threshold. While this seems to be a valid solution, and it is used in several approaches, there are two important complications.

- Since the amount of errors in data is usually unknown, identifying a suitable threshold to overcome the noise is a trial-and-error process, where several thresholds are tried until an appropriate value is identified. In our running example, we would have to put a 20% threshold to discover R_2 (r_3 is one tuple among five).
- Even after setting a threshold, it is not guaranteed that the rules mined out of the frequent patterns are semantically valid. In fact, large thresholds lead to rules that are incorrect. For example, if we set the noise threshold to 20% in Fig. 2, a DC discovery algorithm would mine rule R_5

$$\forall T_\alpha, T_\beta \in R, \neg(T_\alpha.Desc. = T_\beta.Desc. \wedge T_\alpha.Type \neq T_\beta.Type)$$

This is because we treat as error the evidence from tuple r_1 that in "AZ", "Shoes" are allowed to be categorized as "Grocery" items. An appropriate rule would have been

$$\forall T_\alpha, T_\beta \in R, \neg(T_\alpha.Location = T_\beta.Location \wedge T_\alpha.Description =$$
$$T_\beta.Description \wedge T_\alpha.Type \neq T_\beta.Type)$$

but this is not inferred because the incorrect rule is more general, and for implication the correct rule is not part of the output.

Large Output. Consider again the example in Fig. 2. A possible rule would state that ItemID equals to "9286" indicates "EarPhones". If we go beyond comparisons based on equalities, we could incorrectly infer that items with a description of "EarPhones" and ItemID greater than "9286" are classified with type "General". Experiments show that temporal FDs are most effective if the duration constants are discovered at the entity level by defining a rule with different constants for each entity [1]. For instance, Obama travels more often than an average person, and therefore has a smaller duration in the "same time" example discussed above. The same observation motivated Conditional Functional Dependencies, which extend FDs with constants. It is easy to see that there is a plethora of rules pivoting on constants, and the good ones are hidden among the many that do not hold semantically. The traditional way to handle this big search space is to rely on the most popular constants [1,10]. These constants occur in enough tuples to gather the evidence to derive a rule. This support threshold to mine rules containing only popular constants is a crucial parameter in the input definition to find the sweet spot between acceptable execution times and the discovery of useful rules involving constants.

Enabling constants leads to a large number of rules in the output of the mining systems. To facilitate the users, implication tests for pruning and ranking techniques are popular solutions. However, ranking rules is hard, as useful, correct rules may have very low support, i.e., since they cover only very few tuples for rare events, therefore they may end up at the bottom of the ranking. Other systems resort even to crowdsourcing as a post-processing step to evaluate the rules [11,32]. However, the results are commonly in the order of thousands of rules, thus hard to skim, especially when most of the discovered rules are not useful because of the issues raised by the approximation that handles the noise. Ultimately, selecting the correct rules among thousands of results is a daunting task that requires experts both in the rule language at hand (to understand the precise semantics of the rule: "what does it mean?") and in the data domain (to validate the semantic correctness of the rule: "is it always true?").

Hard Configuration. As it should be clear from the discussion on the role of noise and constants, rule discovery algorithms require several non-obvious parameters to be set. In general, there is no way to know in advance what is the amount of noise that should be tolerated in the discovery of the rules. Also, high noise threshold can hide important rules, so there is no one unique value that suddenly leads to the discovery of all the semantically correct rules. The same challenge applies for the threshold for the constant values and several other parameters that are language specific. For example, in algorithms for the discovery of TFDs the granularity of the time buckets is required (minutes, hours, or days?) [1], or for inference rules mining, the maximum number of hops to be traversed in the KB must be set [16].

Since the search space of possible rules is exponential in the number of attributes, some systems even require an initial suggestion of the rule structure from the user to begin with. For instance, in [33], the user is asked to provide the DNF specification of the rule grammar for Entity Resolution that specifies the attributes that need to be considered to classify a pair of tuples as referring to the same entity or not. In addition to that, in case the rules rely on functions with accompanying thresholds, it is a difficult task for the user to specify those values (how similar should two IDs be to be considered a match?).

Need for Heterogeneous Rule Types. Several types of rules are needed for any application, but there is no a single system that discovers all kinds of rules [2]. There are primarily two different types of rules - syntactic and semantic. The error that we see in tuple r_3 of Fig. 2 can be fixed by a semantic rule, such as a DC that states that "EarPhones" can be tagged as a "General" item in all states but "WA" (R_2). But a regular expression that restrains the text patterns in the table in Fig. 2 would capture if an entry for Location is expressed as "Washington", instead of "WA". Likewise, if another syntactic rule states that ItemID can only be a 5-digit number, tuple r_5 can be treated as a violation of that rule because of the 4-digit entry for $ItemID$. Specific tools such as Trifacta [18] and OpenRefine [2] discover and enforce syntactic rules as regular expressions on the textual patterns of the attribute values. The same discussion applies for lookup rules. There can be data errors that are not captured syntactically nor by a DC, but require to verify the data with some reference information, such as in R_7 (Sect. 2.2), but these rules usually require different discovery algorithms (e.g., [11,14]).

It is clear that in general more than one rule type needs to be defined for a given application. But this implies that multiple tools need to be configured and multiple outputs must be manually verified by the users.

3   Opportunities and Directions

To overcome the challenges in Sect. 2, we envision a rule discovery system that puts the users at the center of the mining process. The main idea is that the human-in-the-loop proactively participates in the discovery by interacting with the mining algorithms, instead of limiting the interaction to the specification of parameters and the post-pruning of rules emitted by the black box. Following are the main directions of research that we recognize in recent work for the new generation of rule discovery systems.

Continuous Involvement. Given the challenges discussed in the previous section, we argue that there is a clear opportunity of having the human expert involved along with the system in the rule generation process. This means that the users do not need to set up the parameters upfront, and do not need to evaluate long lists of rules at the output. However, the first step to move toward this vision is to achieve interactive response times in the mining steps. There have been several efforts to reduce the overall mining time by exploiting distributed algorithms [7, 19]. These solutions exploit parallelization techniques to distribute the most expensive operations, such as joins, by using native primitives under the Map-Reduce paradigm. However, we argue that another direction should be explored to enable a novel, more effective approach to the rule discovery problem.

The solution we envision for this problem is to drop the one-shot algorithms that discover all the possible rules in a dataset. Instead, we should interleave the pivotal steps of the rule mining algorithm with user interactions. Of course, understanding when and how to ask for user feedback is a crucial requirement. Recent works have started to look at this problem in the context of user updates [17, 18]. The systems discover the possible rules underlying a given update and validate the most promising tentative rules with the users. This early feedback is useful to prune large portions of the search space and guide the algorithms towards the correct rules. Besides that, pivoting on the user for feedback can also address the issue of *noise*, even when the examples underlying meaningful rules have very small support in the table, such as tuple r_1 in Fig. 2. In this example, a single tuple is below the noise threshold and can hence be mistaken for noise. However such an example can be championed by the data expert is (s)he thinks that the corresponding rule can contribute to high coverage and recall.

Let us clarify this idea of contribution in the context of data cleaning. For data cleaning rules, the challenge lies in identifying the rule that maximizes the number of covered dirty tuples in the database, while minimizing the number of questions asked to the users. Given a search space of the possible rules, the algorithms try to quickly identify rules to be presented to the user for validation that are both as general as possible (to maximize impact) and most likely correct (to quickly identify valid rules). This is in opposition to the enumeration of the entire space of traditional algorithms. Results show that with as little as two questions for a user update, general rules can be discovered [17]. This is done from a user update, a simple action that does not require setting input parameters. By validating a small number of "promising" rules with the user (i.e., rules that find the good compromise between coverage and likelihood of being correct), the system is not exposing the long list of rules to evaluate at the end of a time consuming mining. Thus the algorithmic effort in presenting the right set of questions to the human-in-the-loop coupled with her feedback tackle the issue of the *large output*.

For example, consider again Fig. 2. If the user updates the incorrect value "General" to "Electronics", this would create a search space with Type as the right hand side of the rule, as this is where the user made the update. Now the search space is still exponential over the number of attributes, but with the user validating or refusing a possible rule, the algorithm quickly converges to the search space area containing the correct rule. Suppose the first rule exposed to the user is

$$\forall T_\alpha \in R, \neg(T_\alpha.Desc. = \text{``EarPhones''} \wedge T_\alpha.Type \neq \text{``Electronics''})$$

and the user does not validate it. This is a clear sign that a more specific rule is needed, if we want to use Description. So another question can be asked for rule

$$\forall T_\alpha \in R, \neg(T_\alpha.Loc. = \text{``AZ''} \wedge T_\alpha.Desc. = \text{``EarPhones''} \wedge T_\alpha.Type \neq \text{``Electronics''})$$

which this time is validated. A rule involving constants is obtained for a dirty dataset without setting any input parameter.

However, two important limitations hinder the impact of such solutions. First, the current languages support simple 1-tuple rules, thus not exploiting more powerful rule languages, such as Denial Constraints over multiple tuples. Second, these systems are designed to handle one update at a time, or a sequence of updates with the same semantics. However, given a batch of user updates over the data, such as historical data for data cleaning, it is rarely the case that all updates have been made with a single rule in mind. On the contrary, it is likely that each, or subsets, of the updates have a different underlying rule guiding the users towards the update. This is a challenging problem for which new algorithms are needed.

	ItemID	Location	Title	Description	Type
r_1	-	AZ	Levis.D	Shoes	General
r_1'	-	Arizona	L.Denim	Shoes	FootWear
r_2	34987	California	AllStar	Shoes	FootWear
r_2'	-	CA	Converse.AS	Shoes	FootWear

Fig. 3. De-duplicating items in a grocery store.

User Defined Functions. As discussed above, more expressive rules are needed in real world datasets for complex problems, such as de-duplication (a.k.a., entity resolution) [6,23,30]. For instance, if we treat r_1 and r_1' as a tuple pair in Fig. 3, we may want to be able to assess whether the records in the pair are duplicates of the same item.

An approach to the de-duplication problem is to feed ML algorithms with positive and negative examples, and build a model for a classifier. Interestingly, a set of rules can outperform an ML based approach for this task [30,33]. In particular, provided a grammar to shape the form of the rules and a library of similarity functions (available also to the ML classifier), the appropriate functions and their thresholds can be automatically discovered given sets of positive and negative pairs. In our example in Fig. 3, a DNF grammar can be

$$sim(ItemID) \vee (sim(Title) \wedge sim(Type)) \vee (sim(Title) \wedge sim(Loc.) \wedge sim(Desc.))$$

The rules satisfying this grammar state that a tuple pair can be labeled identical if the tuples are similar w.r.t. ItemID alone (expressed by *sim* function), or over Title and Type together, or upon Title, Location, and Description. However, the ItemID values are often missing from the table in Fig. 3, which makes other DNF clauses in the grammar more useful in this example. Given a library of similarity functions $F_1, \ldots, F_n$ and a set of threshold values $T_1, \ldots, T_m$, the computation of similarity function $sim(attr)$ in the DNF grammar is done by checking every $F_i(r_1[attr], r_1'[attr]) > T_j$, with $i \in 1, \ldots, n$ and $j \in 1, \ldots, m$. The test checks if the outcome of applying the similarity function F_i upon the attribute *attr* exceeds one or more threshold values. The system then picks the appropriate F_i and T_j for all attributes participating in the DNF grammar by pruning redundant threshold values and similarity functions with greedy and hill climbing algorithms.

This is a case of the opportunity of using a library of UDFs to discover more expressive rules, without exposing the internals of the mining to the domain experts. The system is thus not *hard to configure* as all the human helper needs to provide is an easy-to-define input in the form of labeled training data and has to examine the results matches and mismatches, which can be used to refine the rules, rather than the output rules themselves. As in the case of the updates, users only have to deal with examples over the data, thus there is no required expertise in logic nor in procedural code. However, in cases where the training sets are too small or not representative, the above approach would fail. It is easy to see *active learning* as a tool to help classify ambiguous test data by using human support. Bootstrapping hard-to-classify test points into the training data will strengthen the rule mining algorithms. Tuple r_1 in Fig. 2 is a hard-to-classify example as it is mistaken for an error by most rule discovery systems. A human may know that stores in "AZ" should classify "Shoes" as "General" items, thus she would label this tuple as a candidate into the training data. However, integrating active learning to the discovery process is not easy because new mining algorithms should be designed for identifying what are the most beneficial examples for the internal model. While this has shown potential in ad-hoc solutions [29], it is not obvious how to make it more general for the discovery of arbitrary rules beyond entity resolution.

Tool Ensembles. Given the necessity of using a plethora of *heterogeneous rules* to fix multiple types of errors, an ensemble of tools performs better than a single tool. Recent results have shown that combining multiple kinds of rules is mandatory to obtain high recall in the task at hand, and best results are obtained when combining rules with statistical methods [2, 27]. For example, a recent ensemble for error detection in [2] consists of tools for outlier detection together with both syntactic and semantic rules. The authors here focus on combining the cleaning suggestions from these tools over the data, as they rely on manually tuned tools and *hand written rules*.

However, we know that discovering correct rules is a challenging problem, and (manually) doing it over dirty data for multiple tools is indeed an expensive operation. To tackle this problem, we believe that the idea of assembling different rules should be lifted to the idea of combining multiple discovery algorithms. Instead of having the user manually checking rules for each tool supporting a single language (say, syntactic or semantic), the ensemble over the data enables a unified approach to the heterogeneity problem. Given multiple algorithms to discover rules on a given dataset, we can filter the rules emitted by the ensemble to apply only those that have a mutual consensus about identifying a tuple or an attribute for the task at hand. This naive approach is similar to majority voting – if a large fraction of algorithms agree, then they are trustable –but more sophisticated techniques can be developed. For example, the majority voting can be parameterized by using a *min-K* approach, where K indicates the minimum number of tools that produce rules that agree over the data. Another approach resorts to ordering the diverse rules from the ensemble by their estimated precision, for example computed upon a sampled dataset for which the ground truth is available. This enables a data expert to validate the outcome emitted by each tool in the ranked order, while implicitly giving feedback on all the rule discovery algorithms. In fact, we can label the rules as meaningful or not depending on the validation of the rule outcome by the expert. This ensures that a manual validation step can greatly help the rule selection.

4   Conclusion

Discovering rules that are semantically meaningful is important in many applications, but it is a challenging task. In this paper, we propose to open the black box of rule discovery systems to the end user by emphasizing the need to employ early human feedback into the rule mining process. There are techniques that also aim at opening the blackbox of Machine Learning for Information Extraction (IE) [9]. However, ML approaches are mostly non-interpretable.

Our vision goes beyond the state-of-the-art rule mining frameworks that use the human help only to set parameters and to select valid rules from the discovered ones. We argue that such design decisions fail to effectively help the users in producing meaningful rules. This goal can be better achieved by enabling human suggestions during the algorithmic phase of rule discovery.

In this context, we discussed how recent trends in rule discovery systems show great potential for new research that finally put the user at the center of the mining process. We advocate for new solutions with the goal of graciously involving the human in the mining, with very limited input to bootstrap and immediate interaction to guide the mining towards the right direction. The three main directions that we advocate are (i) a direct involvement of the user in the traversal of the search space, (ii) the support for libraries of user defined functions to discover more expressive rules, and (iii) an ensemble of rule discovery algorithms to handle the diversity of languages available and steer effectively the human interaction.

References

1. Abedjan, Z., Akcora, C.G., Ouzzani, M., Papotti, P., Stonebraker, M.: Temporal rules discovery for web data cleaning. Proc. VLDB Endow. **9**(4), 336–347 (2015)
2. Abedjan, Z., Chu, X., Deng, D., Fernandez, R.C., Ilyas, I.F., Ouzzani, M., Papotti, P., Stonebraker, M., Tang, N.: Detecting data errors: Where are we and what needs to be done? Proc. VLDB Endow. **9**(12), 993–1004 (2016)
3. Agrawal, R., Imieliński, T., Swami, A.: Mining association rules between sets of items in large databases. SIGMOD Rec. **22**(2), 207–216 (1993)
4. Bhatla, T.P., Prabhu, V., Dua, A.: Understanding credit card frauds. In Cards Business Review 1.6 (2003)
5. Brause, R., Langsdorf, T., Hepp, M.: Neural data mining for credit card fraud detection. In: ICTAI (1999)
6. Chardin, B., Coquery, E., Pailloux, M., Petit, J.-M.: RQL: a query language for rule discovery in databases. Theoretical Computer Science, November 2016
7. Chen, Y., Goldberg, S., Wang, D.Z., Johri, S.S.: Ontological pathfinding: mining first-order knowledge from large knowledge bases. In: SIGMOD, pp. 835–846. ACM (2016)
8. Chiang, F., Miller, R.J.: Discovering data quality rules. PVLDB **1**(1), 1166–1177 (2008)
9. Chiticariu, L., Li, Y., Reiss, F.: Transparent machine learning for information extraction. In: EMNLP (tutorial) (2015)
10. Chu, X., Ilyas, I.F., Papotti, P.: Discovering denial constraints. Proc. VLDB Endow. **6**(13), 1498–1509 (2013)
11. Chu, X., Morcos, J., Ilyas, I.F., Ouzzani, M., Papotti, P., Tang, N., Ye, Y.: KATARA: a data cleaning system powered by knowledge bases and crowdsourcing. In: SIGMOD (2015)
12. Dieng, C.T., Jen, T.-Y., Laurent, D., Spyratos, N.: Mining frequent conjunctive queries using functional and inclusion dependencies. VLDB J. **22**(2), 125–150 (2013)
13. Fan, W., Geerts, F., Li, J., Xiong, M.: Discovering conditional functional dependencies. IEEE TKDE **23**(5), 683–698 (2011)
14. Fan, W., Li, J., Ma, S., Tang, N., Yu, W.: Towards certain fixes with editing rules and master data. VLDB J. **21**(2), 213–238 (2012)

15. Furche, T., Gottlob, G., Libkin, L., Orsi, G., Paton, N.W.: Data wrangling for big data: challenges and opportunities. In: EDBT, pp. 473–478 (2016)
16. Galárraga, L., Teflioudi, C., Hose, K., Suchanek, F.M.: Fast rule mining in ontological knowledge bases with AMIE+. VLDB J. **24**(6), 707–730 (2015)
17. He, J., Veltri, E., Santoro, D., Li, G., Mecca, G., Papotti, P., Tang, N.: Interactive and deterministic data cleaning. In: SIGMOD (2016)
18. Heer, J., Hellerstein, J., Kandel, S.: Predictive interaction for data transformation. In: CIDR (2015)
19. Heise, A., Quiané-Ruiz, J.-A., Abedjan, Z., Jentzsch, A., Naumann, F.: Scalable discovery of unique column combinations. Proc. VLDB Endow. **7**(4), 301–312 (2013)
20. Hu, B., Patkos, T., Chibani, A., Amirat, Y.: Rule-based context assessment in smart cities. In: Web Reasoning and Rule Systems: RR, pp. 221–224 (2012)
21. Huhtala, Y., Kärkkäinen, J., Porkka, P., Toivonen, H.: TANE: an efficient algorithm for discovering functional and approximate dependencies. Comput. J. **42**(2), 100–111 (1999)
22. Julisch, K., Dacier, M.: Mining intrusion detection alarms for actionable knowledge. In: KDD, pp. 366–375 (2002)
23. Khayyat, Z., Ilyas, I.F., Jindal, A., Madden, S., Ouzzani, M., Quiane-Ruiz, J.-A., Papotti, P., Tang, N., Yin, S.: BigDansing: a system for big data cleansing. In: SIGMOD (2015)
24. Milo, T., Novgorodov, S., Tan, W.-C.: RUDOLF: interactive rule refinement system for fraud detection. Proc. VLDB Endow. **9**(13), 1465–1468 (2016)
25. Naumann, F., Herschel, M.: An Introduction to Duplicate Detection. Synthesis Lectures on Data Management. Morgan & Claypool Publishers, San Rafael (2010)
26. Papenbrock, T., Ehrlich, J., Marten, J., Neubert, T., Rudolph, J., Schönberg, M., Zwiener, J., Naumann, F.: Functional dependency discovery: an experimental evaluation of seven algorithms. PVLDB **8**(10), 1082–1093 (2015)
27. Prokoshyna, N., Szlichta, J., Chiang, F., Miller, R.J., Srivastava, D.: Combining quantitative and logical data cleaning. Proc. VLDB Endow. **9**(4), 300–311 (2015)
28. Roesch, M.: SNORT - Lightweight intrusion detection for networks. In: LISA, pp. 229–238 (1999)
29. Sarawagi, S., Bhamidipaty, A.: Interactive deduplication using active learning. In: SIGKDD, pp. 269–278 (2002)
30. Singh, R., Meduri, V., Elmagarmid, A.K., Madden, S., Papotti, P., Quiané-Ruiz, J., Solar-Lezama, A., Tang, N.: Generating concise entity matching rules. In: SIGMOD, pp. 1635–1638 (2017)
31. Song, S., Chen, L., Cheng, H.: Efficient determination of distance thresholds for differential dependencies. IEEE Trans. Knowl. Data Eng. **26**(9), 2179–2192 (2014)
32. Suganthan, P., Sun, C., Gayatri, K., Zhang, H., Yang, F., Rampalli, N., Prasad, S., Arcaute, E., Krishnan, G., Deep, R., Raghavendra, V., Doan, A.: Why big data industrial systems need rules and what we can do about it. In: SIGMOD, pp. 265–276 (2015)
33. Wang, J., Li, G., Yu, J.X., Feng, J.: Entity matching: how similar is similar. Proc. VLDB Endow. **4**(10), 622–633 (2011)
34. Wyss, C., Giannella, C., Robertson, E.: FastFDs: a heuristic-driven, depth-first algorithm for mining functional dependencies from relation instances extended abstract. In: Kambayashi, Y., Winiwarter, W., Arikawa, M. (eds.) DaWaK 2001. LNCS, vol. 2114, pp. 101–110. Springer, Heidelberg (2001). doi:10.1007/3-540-44801-2_11

Discovering Injective Mapping
Between Relations in Astrophysics Databases

Nicu-Razvan Stancioiu[1], Lhouari Nourine[2], Jean-Marc Petit[1(⊠)],
Vasile-Marian Scuturici[1], Dominique Fouchez[4], Emmanuel Gangler[3],
and Philippe Gris[3]

[1] Université de Lyon, CNRS, INSA-Lyon, LIRIS,
UMR5205, 69621 Villeurbanne, France
{nicu.stancioiu,jean-marc.petit,marian.scuturici}@insa-lyon.fr
[2] Clermont-Université, Université Blaise Pascal, LIMOS, CNRS,
Clermont-Ferrand, France
nourine@isima.fr
[3] Clermont-Université, LPC, CNRS, Clermont-Ferrand, France
emmanuel.gangler@clermont.in2p3.fr
[4] IN2P3, CNRS, Marseile, France
fouchez@cppm.in2p3.fr

Abstract. Data in Astrophysics are very often structured with the relational data model. One particularity is that every value is a real number and comes with an associated error measure, leading to a numerical interval $[value - error, value + error]$. Such Astrophysics databases can be seen as *interval-based numerical databases*.

Classical data mining approach, specifically those related to integrity constraints, are likely to produce useless results on such databases, as the strict equality is very unlikely to give meaningful results.

In this paper, we revisit a well-known problem, based on unary inclusion dependency discovery, to match the particularities of Astrophysics Databases. We propose to discover injective mapping between attributes of a source relation and a target relation. At first, we define two notions of inclusion between intervals. Then, we adapt a condensed representation proposed in [15] allowing to find a mapping function between the source and the target. The proposition has been implemented and several experiments have been conducted on both real-life and synthetic databases.

1 Introduction

Astrophysics is known to generate huge amount of data in large experiments, as for example with the Large Synoptic Survey Telescope (LSST[1]), a wide-field survey reflecting telescope in Chile. The camera is expected to take over 500,000 pictures per year, leading to more than 60 petabytes of data at the end of the project. After a long image processing process, relevant data are stored in

---

[1] https://www.lsst.org.

© Springer International Publishing AG 2017
D. Kotzinos et al. (Eds.): ISIP 2016, CCIS 760, pp. 18–32, 2017.
DOI: 10.1007/978-3-319-68282-2_2

d	u	g	r	i	z	err_u	err_g	err_r	err_i	err_z
t_1 :	23.37	24.52	23.42	24.27	20.76	0.52	0.52	0.43	0.73	0.21
t_2 :	18.44	16.33	15.48	15.20	15.07	0.01	0.01	0.01	0.02	0.01
t_3 :	23.77	22.85	23.39	22.41	22.60	0.77	0.16	0.41	0.29	0.76
t_4 :	22.72	20.88	19.51	18.79	18.41	0.43	0.03	0.01	0.01	0.03
t_5 :	22.48	21.82	21.38	21.17	21.25	0.24	0.07	0.06	0.07	0.29
t_6 :	24.04	20.99	19.68	19.10	18.84	0.77	0.03	0.01	0.01	0.03

Fig. 1. Example of astrophysics database

specialized Relational Database Management Systems (RDBMS). Since every value comes with its associated error measure, it can be seen as a numerical interval $[value - error, value + error]$. Then, such Astrophysics databases are *interval-based numerical databases* and look like the data given in Fig. 1. u and err_u (resp. g, r, i, z) are the magnitude (flux in log scale) and corresponding error of an astrophysical object measured through a passband color filter named u (resp. g, r, i, z). The u, g, r, i, z color filters slice the visible spectrum in five similar size bins. For each attribute that contains a magnitude parameter, there is an associated error measure attribute (e.g. u and err_u).

Classical data mining approach, specifically those related to integrity constraints like functional dependencies (FD), conditional FD or inclusion dependencies (IND), are likely to produce useless results on such databases. The particularities of interval-based databases impose peculiar problems to the associated discovery problems.

In this paper, we revisit a well-known problem, the discovery of unary inclusion dependency discovery, to match the particularities of Astrophysics Databases. Due to the nature of the data in use, the proposed solution has to be changed with respect to existing approaches [15, 16].

More precisely, we propose to discover injective mapping between attributes of a source relation and a target relation. In order to solve the problem of discovering such mappings, we adapt the problem of discovering unary inclusion dependencies for interval-based databases. With respect to the application domain in Astrophysics, we do not claim that such mappings solve real problems for astrophysicists, even if some applications could benefit from it. The problem studied in this paper should be thought as a first step, opening many opportunities to address others related problems, more challenging and interesting for astrophysicists.

Let us consider two interval-based relations s and t over relation schema S and T respectively. As usual, attributes of a relation r over R are denoted by $sch(R)$.

Problem Statement

Given a source s and a target t such that $|sch(S)| \leq |sch(T)|$, find a mapping f from $sch(S)$ to $sch(T)$ such that (1) f is injective ($f(A) = f(B) \Rightarrow A = B$) and (2) for every attribute $A \in sch(R)$, the values of A

in s and the values of $f(A)$ in t should be as similar as possible, i.e. some forms of inclusion dependencies should exist between them.

To deal with this problem, we propose a contribution based on the following three-step process:

- First, we define two types of membership of an interval into a collection of intervals. The first one is based on the classical inclusion between intervals while the second one is defined on the so-called *canonical representation* of a collection of intervals.
- Second, we extend the work of [15] and build a condensed representation of an interval-based numerical database as a binary relation (or transactional database where transactions are values and items are attributes). At the end, we discover a set of approximate unary inclusion dependencies from the source to the target.
- Finally, we propose a method to find an injective mapping, which is equivalent to the minimum weight matching in an weighted bipartite graph, resolved with the *Hungarian* algorithm [12] in this paper.

The proposition has been implemented and several experiments have been conducted on both real-life and synthetic databases. Even if the overall complexity of the studied problem remains polynomial, the overhead with respect to classical databases turns out to be rather low. The main lesson we have learned from this work is that many contributions in pattern mining could be revisited in order to deal with interval-based numerical databases.

To the best of our knowledge, this is the first contribution dealing with the discovery of integrity constraints in interval-based numerical databases.

Paper Organization. The remaining part of the paper is organized as follows: Sect. 2 gives preliminaries of the paper. Section 3 adapts the condensed representation of [15] to interval-based databases. Section 4 introduces details about the discovery of approximate unary inclusion dependencies. Section 5 describes the main algorithm *SR2TR* providing an injective mapping between a source and a target relations, and the results of experiments. Section 7 concludes the paper and gives some perspectives to this work.

2   Preliminaries

Basic database notions are given here, more details can be found for example in [14]. We restrict our attention to interval-based numerical databases only.

Let $\mathcal{U}$ be a set of attributes and $\mathcal{D}$ the possible intervals over real numbers. A relation symbol is generally denoted by R and its schema by $sch(R), sch(R) \subseteq \mathcal{U}$. When clear from context, we shall use R instead of $sch(R)$. Each attribute has a domain, included in $\mathcal{D}$. A tuple over R is an element of the cartesian product $\mathcal{D}^{|R|}$. An interval-based numerical relation (or simply relation) r over R is a set of tuples over R. An interval-based numerical database d (or simply database) over a set of relation symbol $\{R_1, \ldots, R_n\}$ is a set of n interval-based relations $\{r_1, \ldots, r_n\}$, r_i defined over R_i for $i = 1..n$.

Given a relation r over R and $A \in R$, the active domain of A in r is denoted by $ADOM(A, r)$. The active domain of r is denoted by $ADOM(r) = \bigcup_{A \in R} ADOM(A, r)$. The projection of a tuple t on an attribute set $X \subseteq R$ is denoted by $t[X]$. The projection of a relation r onto a set of attributes X, denoted by $\pi_X(r)$, is defined by $\pi_X(r) = \{t[X] | t \in r\}$.

Let I, J be two intervals of $\mathcal{D}$. We note $min(I)$ (resp. $max(I)$) the minimum (resp. maximum) value of I. I is contained in J, denoted by $I \subseteq J$, if $min(J) \leq min(I) \leq max(I) \leq max(J)$.

Let $\mathcal{I}$ be a collection of intervals of $\mathcal{D}$. The union of $\mathcal{I}$ is the minimal number of intervals covering $\mathcal{I}$. Since its union is unique, it represents a canonical form of $\mathcal{I}$, and will be denoted by $cano(\mathcal{I})$. More formally, $cano(\mathcal{I})$ can be defined by induction as follows:

$$
\begin{aligned}
cano(\mathcal{I}) &= \mathcal{I} && \text{if for all } J_1, J_2 \in \mathcal{I}, J_1 \cap J_2 = \emptyset \\
&= cano(\mathcal{I} \setminus \{J_1, J_2\}) \cup \{J_3\}) && \text{otherwise with } J_1, J_2 \in \mathcal{I}, J_1 \cap J_2 \neq \emptyset \text{ and} \\
&&& J_3 = [min(min(J_1), min(J_2)), max(max(J_1), max(J_2))]
\end{aligned}
$$

$\mathcal{I}$ is said to be *connected* if $|cano(\mathcal{I})| = 1$.

We now introduce the classical syntax and semantics of unary inclusion dependencies between relation symbols R and S.

Definition 1. *An unary inclusion dependency (UIND) from R to S is a statement of the form $R[A] \subseteq S[B]$, where $A \in R$, $B \in S$.*

Definition 2. *Let $d = \{r, s\}$ be a database over $\{R, S\}$. An unary inclusion dependency $R[A] \subseteq S[B]$ is satisfied in d, denoted by $d \models R[A] \subseteq S[B]$, iff for all $u \in r$, there is $v \in s$ such that $u[A] = v[B]$ or equivalently $\pi_A(r) \subseteq \pi_B(s)$.*

Example 1. Let r_0 be a classical relation over R (see Fig. 2).

Several classical UINDs are satisfied in $\{r_0\}$, for instance $R[A] \subseteq R[D]$ and $R[B] \subseteq R[C]$.

r_0	A	B	C	D
t_1	0	1	1	2
t_2	1	2	2	1
t_3	2	1	1	0

Fig. 2. A toy relation r_0

When working with intervals, the strict equality "$=$" used in the definition of the satisfaction of an UIND is likely to produce unsatisfying results. For instance, in Fig. 3, the relation r_1 has no satisfied UINDs.

This leads to introducing different UIND satisfaction on intervals.

We define two kinds of satisfied UINDs over interval-based numerical database: *classical satisfaction* based on interval inclusion over collection of intervals and

r_1	A	B	C
t_1 :	[0,0.5]	[0,1]	[0,1.5]
t_2 :	[1,1.5]	[1,2]	[3,3.5]
t_3 :	[2,3]	[1.5,4]	[2,3]

Fig. 3. A toy interval-based relation r_1

canonical satisfaction based on interval inclusion over the canonical representation of collection of intervals.

Let $d = \{r, s\}$ be an interval-based numerical database over $\{R, S\}$.

Definition 3. *An UIND $R[A] \subseteq S[B]$ is classically satisfied in d, denoted by $d \models_1 R[A] \subseteq S[B]$, iff for all $u \in r$, there is $v \in s$ such that $u[A] \subseteq v[B]$.*

An UIND $R[A] \subseteq S[B]$ is canonically satisfied in d, denoted by $d \models_2 R[A] \subseteq S[B]$, iff for all $u \in r$, there is $v \in cano(ADOM(B, s))$ such that $u[A] \subseteq v$.

We will note $d \models_\lambda R[A] \subseteq S[B]$ to refer to both of them.

Example 2. In the relation r_1 of Fig. 3, for the satisfaction, we have an UIND $r_0 \models A \subseteq_1 B$ as $[0, 0.5] \subseteq [0, 1]$, $[1, 1.5] \subseteq [1, 2]$ and $[2, 3] \subseteq [1.5, 4]$. For the second one, $r_0 \models A \subseteq_2 B$ as $[0, 0.5] \subseteq [0, 4]$, $[1, 1.5] \subseteq [0, 4]$ and $[2, 3] \subseteq [0, 4]$.

We also need to define when a given interval belongs to a collection of intervals.

Let I be an interval and $\mathcal{I}$ a collection of intervals.

I is classically *included* in $\mathcal{I}$, denoted by $I \subseteq_1 \mathcal{I}$, if there exists $I' \in \mathcal{I}$ such that $I \subseteq I'$. I is canonically *included* in $\mathcal{I}$, denoted by $I \subseteq_2 \mathcal{I}$ if $I \subseteq_1 cano(\mathcal{I})$.

3 Condensed Representation for Interval-Based Relations

We now extend the contribution for discovering UINDs in databases [15] to interval-based numerical databases. This is, up to our knowledge, the best approach for discovering UINDs. It relies on a preprocessing to get a condensed representation from the initial database.

Now, we define a condensed representation for UIND discovery.

Definition 4. *The condensed representation of an interval-based numerical relation r, denoted by $CR_{\subseteq_\lambda}(r)$, is defined by:*

$$CR_{\subseteq_\lambda}(r) = \{(I, X) \mid I \in ADOM(r), X = \{A \in R \mid I \subseteq_\lambda ADOM(A, r)\}\}$$

Condensed representations from the two defined satisfactions can be different. We denote $CR_{\subseteq_1}(r)$ and $CR_{\subseteq_2}(r)$ the condensed representations for $\subseteq_1$ and $\subseteq_2$ respectively.

Example 3. The condensed representations $CR_{\subseteq_1}(r_1)$ and $CR_{\subseteq_2}(r_1)$ of the relation r_1 (see Fig. 3).

$CR_{\subseteq_1}(r_1)$		$CR_{\subseteq_2}(r_1)$	
[0,0.5]	ABC	[0,0.5]	ABC
[1,1.5]	ABC	[1,1.5]	ABC
[2,3]	ABC	[2,3]	ABC
[0,1]	BC	[0,1]	BC
[1,2]	B	[1,2]	B
[1.5,4]	B	[1.5,4]	B
[0,1.5]	C	[0,1.5]	BC
[3,3.5]	BC	[3,3.5]	BC

Fig. 4. Condensed representations of r_1 for both semantics

Given a set of relations $r_1, r_2, ..., r_n$, its condensed representation is defined by as:

$$CR_{\subseteq_\lambda}(r_1, r_2, ..., r_n) = \bigcup_{i=1..n} CR_{\subseteq_\lambda}(r_i).$$

Definition 5. *The support of an attribute set $X \subseteq R$ in $CR_{\subseteq_\lambda}(r)$, denoted by $sup(X, CR_{\subseteq_\lambda}(r))$, is defined by:*

$$sup(X, CR_{\subseteq_\lambda}(r)) = |\{(i, Y) \in CR_{\subseteq_\lambda}(r) | X \subseteq Y\}|$$

Definition 6. *The closure of an attribute $A \in sch(R)$ with respect to $CR_{\subseteq_\lambda}(r)$, denoted by $A^+_{CR_{\subseteq_\lambda}(r)}$, is defined as:*

$$A^+_{CR_{\subseteq_\lambda}(r)} = \bigcap_{(i,X) \in CR_{\subseteq_\lambda}(r)} \{X | A \in X\}$$

Example 4. In Fig. 4, for $CR_{\subseteq_1}(r_1)$ we have that $sup(\{A\}, CR_{\subseteq_1}(r_1)) = 3$, $sup(\{A, B\}, CR_{\subseteq_1}(r_1)) = 3$ and $A^+_{CR_{\subseteq_1}(r_1)} = \{A, B, C\}$, $C^+_{CR_{\subseteq_1}(r_1)} = \{C\}$. As for $CR_{\subseteq_2}(r_1)$, $sup(\{B, C\}, CR_{\subseteq_2}(r_1)) = 6$, $sup(\{C\}, CR_{\subseteq_2}(r_1)) = 6$ and $C^+_{CR_{\subseteq_2}(r_1)} = \{B, C\}$.

4   Unary Inclusion Dependencies Discovery in a Single Interval-Based Relation

To alleviate the notations, we consider a single relation only, i.e. UIND of the form $r \models_\lambda R[A] \subseteq R[B]$. Let r be a relation over R and $A, B \in R$.

We first give a technical lemma which relates the definition of $r \models_2 A \subseteq B$ to the canonical representation of the intervals of A in r.

Lemma 1. $r \models_2 A \subseteq B \iff \forall I \in cano(ADOM(A,r)), \exists J \in cano(ADOM(B,r)), I \subseteq J$.

Proof. ($\Longrightarrow$) Suppose not. Assume, to the contrary that there exists $I' \in cano(ADOM(A, r))$, such that for all $J \in cano(ADOM(B, r))$, $I' \nsubseteq J$.

Let $\mathcal{I} \subseteq ADOM(A, r)$ be the maximal collection of intervals such that $cano(\mathcal{I}) = \{\mathcal{I}'\}$.

By definition, $r \models_2 A \subseteq B$ implies that for all $I \in ADOM(A, r)$, there exists $J \in cano(ADOM(B, r))$ such that $I \subseteq J$.

If $|\mathcal{I}| = 1$, then we have a contradiction and the result follows.

Assume $|\mathcal{I}| > 1$. The collection $\mathcal{I}$ can be divided into $n > 1$ disjoint non-empty collections of intervals $\{\mathcal{I}_1, \mathcal{I}_2, .., \mathcal{I}_n\}$ such that there exist n different associated intervals $\{J_1, J_2, .., J_n\} \in cano(ADOM(B, r))$ such that for all $I \in \mathcal{I}_\lambda$, $I \subseteq J_\lambda$, $\lambda \in \{1, 2, .., n\}$.

Since $|cano(\mathcal{I})| = 1$, for every $\mathcal{I}_\lambda \in \{\mathcal{I}_1, \mathcal{I}_2, .., \mathcal{I}_n\}$, there exists $\mathcal{I}_{\lambda'} \in \{\mathcal{I}_1, \mathcal{I}_2, .., \mathcal{I}_n\}$, $\lambda \neq \lambda'$ such that there exists $I_0 \in \mathcal{I}_\lambda$, $K_0 \in \mathcal{I}_{\lambda'}$ such that $I_0 \cap K_0 \neq \emptyset$.

But $I_0 \subseteq J_\lambda$, $K_0 \subseteq J_{\lambda'}$, then $J_\lambda \cap J_{\lambda'} \neq \emptyset$. Contradiction as $J_\lambda, J_{\lambda'}$ are supposed to be non-intersecting.

($\Longleftarrow$)

Let $I' \in ADOM(A, r)$. Then there exists $I \in cano(ADOM(A, r))$ such that $I' \subseteq I$. Since for all $I \in cano(ADOM(A, r))$, there exists $J \in cano(ADOM(B, r))$ such that $I \subseteq J$, it follows that $I' \subseteq J$. Thus $r \models_2 A \subseteq B$.

Intuitively, the main result of the paper states that every inclusion of the form $A \subseteq B$ that holds in r turns out to be equivalent to a closure computation on the associated condensed representation.

We can now give the main result of the paper.

Theorem 1.
$$r \models_\lambda A \subseteq B \Longleftrightarrow B \in A^+_{CR_{\subseteq_\lambda}(r)}$$

Proof. We consider the two UIND satisfactions presented before:

1. $r \models_1 A \subseteq B \Longleftrightarrow B \in A^+_{CR_{\subseteq_1}(r)}$

   ($\Longrightarrow$)

   Let $(I', X) \in CR_{\subseteq_1}(r)$ such that $A \in X$. Then, there exists $I \in ADOM(A, r)$ such that $I' \subseteq I$. Or $r \models_1 A \subseteq B$ implies that there exists $J \in ADOM(B, r)$ such that $I \subseteq J$. It follows that $I' \subseteq J$, and thus $B \in X$. Then $B \in A^+_{CR_{\subseteq_1}(r)}$.

   ($\Longleftarrow$)

   $B \in A^+_{CR_{\subseteq_1}(r)} \Longleftrightarrow$ for all $(I, X) \in CR_{\subseteq_1}(r)$, if $A \in X$ then $B \in X$. For all $I \in ADOM(A, r)$, there exists a pair $(I, X) \in CR_{\subseteq_1}(r)$ such that $A \in X$. Thus, $B \in X$ also holds, i.e. there exists $J \in ADOM(B, r)$ such that $I \subseteq J$. Thus $r \models_1 A \subseteq B$.

2. $r \models_2 A \subseteq B \Longleftrightarrow B \in A^+_{CR_{\subseteq_2}(r)}$

   ($\Longrightarrow$)

   Let $(I', X) \in CR_{\subseteq_2}(r)$ such that $A \in X$. Then, there exists $I \in cano(ADOM(A, r))$ such that $I' \subseteq I$. Based on Lemma 1, $r \models_2 A \subseteq B$ implies that there exists $J \in cano(ADOM(B, r))$ such that $I \subseteq J$. It follows that $I' \subseteq J$, and thus $B \in X$. Then $B \in A^+_{CR_{\subseteq_1}(r)}$.

($\Longleftarrow$)

For all $I' \in ADOM(A, r)$, there exists a pair $(I, X) \in CR_{\subseteq_2}(r)$ such that $A \in X$ and $I' \subseteq I$. Thus, $B \in X$ also holds, i.e. there exists $J \in ADOM(B, r)$ such that $I \subseteq J$. It follows that $I' \subseteq J$.

Thus $r \models_2 A \subseteq B$.

From previous theorem, the discovery of UIND is based on the following property, based on support counting in the condensed representation.

Property 1.

$$B \in A^+_{CR_{\subseteq_\lambda}(r)} \Longleftrightarrow sup(\{A, B\}, CR_{\subseteq_\lambda}(r)) = sup(\{A\}, CR_{\subseteq_\lambda}(r)).$$

Proof. $B \in A^+_{CR_{\subseteq_\lambda}(r)} \Longleftrightarrow$ for all $(I, X) \in CR_{\subseteq_\lambda}(r)$, if $A \in X$ then $B \in X$. Equivalently, the support of $\{A\}$ and $\{A, B\}$ are the same in $CR_{\subseteq_\lambda}(r)$, i.e. $sup(\{A, B\}, CR_{\subseteq_\lambda}(r)) = sup(\{A\}, CR_{\subseteq_\lambda}(r))$.

5   Approximate Unary IND Between Two Interval-Based Relations

Within this setting, an unary IND $A\subseteq_\lambda B$ may be still unsatisfied in a relation due to a few counter-examples. As a result, we introduce an approximation measure to extract approximate unary inclusion dependencies from a relation. This approximation will be calculated based on the support of attributes' sets. The error measure related to the correspondence between two attributes, denoted *error* can be defined using the support of attribute sets as follows:

Definition 7. *Let r be a relation over R and $A, B \in R$.*

$$error(r \models_\lambda A \subseteq B) = 1 - \frac{sup(\{A, B\}, CR_{\subseteq_\lambda}(r))}{sup(\{A\}, CR_{\subseteq_\lambda}(r))}$$

Given two relations r over R and s over S, we are interested in finding the approximative unary inclusion dependencies from single attributes of R with respect to singles attributes of S. From now on, we consider the relation r as a *source* relation and s as a *target* relation.

Based on the previous definition we can build a matrix of error measures, such that each element of the matrix is represented as the value of the error measure between a single attribute from R and a single attribute of S (Fig. 5).

Example 5. Let r_2, s_2 be two toy relations:

Based on the condensed representation $CR_{\subseteq_1}(r_2, s_2)$, we build a matrix of error measures $error(\{r_2, s_2\} \models_1 X \subseteq Y)$ with X as attribute over r_2 and Y as attribute over s_2 (Fig. 6):

s_2	D	E	F	G
t_1 :	[0,1.5]	[1,2]	[1.6,1.8]	[2,3]
t_2 :	[0,1.5]	[1,2]	[3.1,4]	[2,3]
t_3 :	[0,1.5]	[0,1]	[0,0.5]	[1,2]
t_4 :	[2,3.5]	[2,3]	[0,0.5]	[1,2]
t_5 :	[2,3.5]	[1,2]	[0,0.5]	[1,2]

r_2	A	B	C
t_1 :	[0,0.5]	[0,1]	[0,1]
t_2 :	[1,1.5]	[1,2]	[3,3.5]
t_3 :	[2,3]	[1.5,4]	[2,3]

Fig. 5. Toy relations r_2 and s_2

$CR_{\subseteq_1}(r_2,s_2)$	
[0,0.5]	ABCDEF
[1,1.5]	ABDEG
[2,3]	ABCDEG
[0,1]	BCDE
[1,2]	BEG
[1.5,4]	B
[3,3.5]	BCD
[0,1.5]	D
[2,3.5]	BD
[1.6,1.8]	BEFG
[3.1,4]	BF

$error(\{r_2,s_2\} \models_1 X \subseteq Y)$	D	E	F	G
A	0.000	0.000	0.667	0.333
B	0.400	0.400	0.700	0.600
C	0.000	0.250	0.750	0.750

Fig. 6. The condensed representation of r_2 and s_2 and the associated matrix of error measures

As we search to find the most appropriate injective matching function between two schema relations, given the matrix of error measures, we can reformulate this problem as follows:

Given an error matrix between two schema relations R and S, find the best matching with the minimum error between R and S.

This problem is in fact an *assignment problem* [12] which consists of finding a maximum weight matching in a weighted bipartite graph. *Hungarian Algorithm* [11] is one of the algorithms that can solve the *assignment problem*. There are other algorithms that include adaptations as the *Simplex Algorithm* and the *Auction Algorithm* [2]. The assignment problem is a special case of the *transportation problem* [10], which is a variation of *minimum cost maximum flow problem* [1].

6   Scalable Algorithms

We propose a polynomial algorithm called $SR2TR$, which provides an injective mapping based on the discovery of a set of approximate unary INDs from a source relation r over R to a target relation s over S.

Algorithm 1. (SR2TR) Mapping from Source Relation to Target Relation

---

Input: two relations: r over R and s over S
Output: A mapping function f from R to S
  1: $CR =$ Preprocessing(r, s)
  2: $M =$ MEM(CR)
  3: $f =$ FindMatching(M)
  4: **return** f.

Algorithm 1 can be summarized as follows:

1. Process the condensed representation $CR(r, s)$ - *Preprocessing(r,s)*;
2. Build the matrix of error measures M based on $CR(r, s)$ - *MEM(CR)*;
3. Find the minimum weight matching in the weighted bipartite graph constructed from M - *FindMatching(M)*.

Two other algorithms are provided: Algorithm 2 for the *Preprocessing* function (line 1 of Algorithm 1) and Algorithm 3 for the *MEM* function (line 2 of Algorithm 1). The *FindMatching* function (line 3, Algorithm 3) corresponds to the *minimum weight matching in a weighted bipartite graph*. From the matrix of error measures M, we have implemented the *Hungarian Algorithm*, not detailed here.

Algorithm 2. (Preprocessing) Computing the condensed representation of $r \cup s$

Input: Two relations r over R and s over S
Output: Condensed representation $CR(r, s)$
  1: $CR = \emptyset$
  2: **for all** $I \in ADOM(r) \cup ADOM(s)$ **do**
  3:     $BR = \emptyset$
  4:     **for all** $A \in R \cup S$ **do**
  5:       **if** $check\_inclusion(I, ADOM(A, r \cup s)) = true$ **then**
  6:         $BR[A] = true$
  7:      **else**
  8:         $BR[A] = false$
  9:      **end if**
10:     **end for**
11:     $CR.add(BR)$
12: **end for**
13: **return** CR

For each interval $I \in ADOM(r) \cup ADOM(s)$, we search all single attributes $A \in R \cup S$ for which I is *included* in $ADOM(A, r \cup s)$ (line 5). Then we update the binary relation BR accordingly, which is afterwards added to CR. As the set $ADOM(A, r \cup s)$ is a set of intervals, from which we can construct an *interval tree* for each single attribute in $R \cup S$, so that *check_inclusion* is logarithmic in the size of the r and s.

Algorithm 3. (MEM) Compute the matrix of error measures

Input: Condensed representation $CR(r, s)$
Output: The matrix of error measures between R and S
1: $init(M)$
2: **for all** $A \in R$ **do**
3:    **for all** $(I, X) \in CR(r, s)$ where $A \in X$ **do**
4:       $sup1[A] = sup1[A] + 1$
5:       **for all** $B \in S$ where $B \in X$ **do**
6:          $sup2[A][B] = sup2[A][B] + 1$
7:       **end for**
8:    **end for**
9: **end for**
10: **for all** $A \in R$ and $B \in S$ **do**
11:    $M[A][B] = 1.0 - sup2[A][B]/sup1[A]$
12: **end for**
13: **return** M

Based on the condensed representation $CR(r, s)$, we form the matrix of error measures M of size $|R| * |S|$. Line 1, M is initialized and filled with zeros in the $init(M)$ function. At this point we create two arrays, $sup1$ and $sup2$, referring to the support of size 1 and 2 of $R \cup S$. Then, we search through all the elements of CR and we update step by step the support accordingly (lines 4, 6). Lines 10–11, we fill the matrix M, such that the value of an element $M[A][B]$ of the matrix is equal to $1 - \frac{sup(\{A,B\})}{sup(\{A\})}$, where $A \in R$ and $B \in S$.

Complexity Analysis of SR2TR. Let $n = |R|$, $m = |S|$, $a = |r|, b = |s|$. The theoretical complexity is in $O((n * a + m * b) * (n * log(a) + m * log(b)) + P)$ where P is the complexity of the matching algorithm. In case of the Hungarian Algorithm, its complexity would be $(n + m)^4$, which can be reduced to $(n + m)^3$ [4,8,9,13].

7   Experimental Results

We implemented the previous algorithms in C++ and conducted experiments to determine its effectiveness. We used datasets provided by astrophysicists of IN2P3 and synthetic databases to check the scalability of the algorithm. Our experiments were run using a machine with an Intel Core i7-4712MQ (2.3 GHz) CPU and 12 GB of memory. We focused on the classical UIND definition, referred to as $\subseteq_1$. The results with canonical UIND, referred to as $\subseteq_2$, being quite similar are not discussed.

The IN2P3 dataset is composed of two databases with 11 single attributes each.

With respect to the number of tuples of the two databases, we obtained acceptable execution times (see Fig. 7), linear in the size of the data.

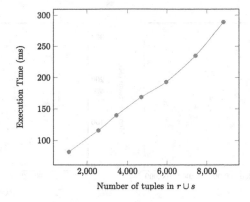

Fig. 7. Real-life astrophysics database

To test the scalability of our technique with regard to the response time and the memory usage, we created 4 tests realized on synthetic datasets. The datasets are composed of floating numbers in the interval $[0, 5000]$ and with an error measure in the interval $[0, 1]$.

The first test considers a target relation of 100000 tuples, 20 attributes in each relation schema and a varying number of tuples in the source relation (see Fig. 8). We can observe a polynomial behavior on experimental results both in response time and memory usage.

The second test considers a source relation of 1000 tuples, 20 attributes in each relation schema and a varying number of tuples in the target relation (see Fig. 9). In both the response time and memory usage we recognize a linear behavior.

The following test considers a target schema relation with 100 single attributes, 100 tuples in each relation and a varying number of single attributes

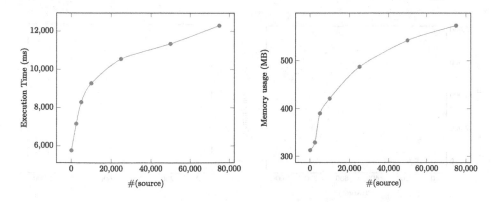

Fig. 8. Varying the number of tuples in the source relation

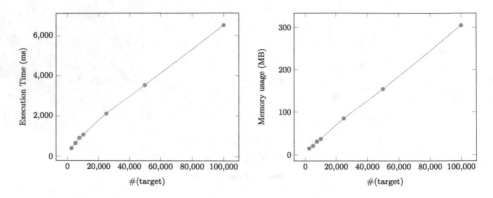

Fig. 9. Varying of the number of tuples in the target relation

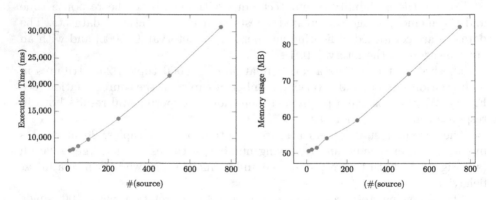

Fig. 10. Varying the number of single attributes in the source schema relation

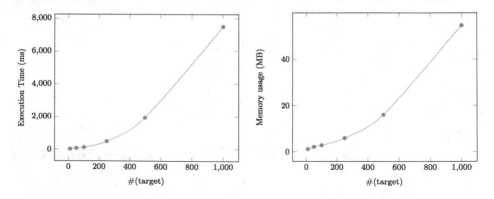

Fig. 11. Varying the number of single attributes in the target schema relation

in the source schema relation (see Fig. 10). We observe a linear behavior on experimental results both in response time and memory usage.

The last test considers a source relation with 10 single attributes, and 100 tuples in each relation and a varying number of single attributes in the target schema relation (see Fig. 11). A polynomial behavior can be observed both in response time and memory usage.

8   Conclusion

We have addressed the problem of finding an injective mapping between attributes from a source relation to a target relation in an interval-based numerical databases. The proposition is mainly based on the work of [15] on the discovery of approximate unary inclusion dependencies. We implemented the contributions and tested on both real life and synthetic databases. Dealing with intervals instead of classical values turns out to feasible in practice for this polynomial problem, and requires mainly to think about notions such as the membership of an interval into a collection of intervals.

Many perspectives do exist for this work: First, the Astrophysics setting of this paper offers opportunities to extend the contributions made in this paper to real Astrophysics problems. More joint works are needed to better understand the needs of each other. Second, many pattern mining problems can be revisited for interval-based numerical databases. For example, the discovery of conditional functional dependencies could be revisited [6] as well as the discovery of editing rules [5,7] for data cleaning, a main concern in Astrophysics.

Acknowledgments. This work has been partially funded by the CNRS Mastodons projects (QualiSky 2016 and 2017).

References

1. Ahuja, R.K., Magnanti, T.L., Orlin, J.B.: Network Flows: Theory, Algorithms, and Applications. Prentice-Hall Inc., Upper Saddle River (1993)
2. Bertsekas, D.P.: A distributed algorithm for the assignment problem (1979)
3. Dantzig, G.B.: Origins of the simplex method. In: Dantzig, G.B. (ed.) A History of Scientific Computing, pp. 141–151. ACM, New York (1990)
4. Dawes, M.: The optimal assignment problem (2012)
5. Diallo, T., Petit, J.-M., Servigne, S.: Discovering editing rules for data cleaning. In: 10th International Workshop on Quality in Databases in Conjunction with VLDB (Very Large Databases), pp. 1–8, August 2012
6. Fan, W., Geerts, F., Li, J., Xiong, M.: Discovering conditional functional dependencies. IEEE Trans. Knowl. Data Eng. **23**(5), 683–698 (2011)
7. Fan, W., Li, J., Ma, S., Tang, N., Yu, W.: Towards certain fixes with editing rules and master data. VLDB J. **21**(2), 213–238 (2012)
8. Golin, M.J.: Bipartite matching and the Hungarian method (2006)
9. Khuller, S.: Design and analysis of algorithms: Course notes (1998)
10. Klein, M.: A primal method for minimal cost flows with applications to the assignment and transportation problems. Manage. Sci. **14**(3), 205–220 (1967)

11. Kuhn, H.W.: The Hungarian method for the assignment problem. Naval Res. Logist. Q. **2**, 83–97 (1955)
12. Kuhn, H.W.: Variants of the Hungarian method for assignment problems. Naval Res. Logist. Q. **3**, 253–258 (1956)
13. Lawler, E.: Combinatorial Optimization: Networks and Matroids. Dover Books on Mathematics Series Mineola. Dover Publications, Mineola (2001)
14. Levene, M., Loizou, G.: A Guided Tour of Relational Databases and Beyond. Springer, London (1999). doi:10.1007/978-0-85729-349-7
15. Marchi, F., Lopes, S., Petit, J.-M.: Efficient algorithms for mining inclusion dependencies. In: Jensen, C.S., Šaltenis, S., Jeffery, K.G., Pokorny, J., Bertino, E., Böhn, K., Jarke, M. (eds.) EDBT 2002. LNCS, vol. 2287, pp. 464–476. Springer, Heidelberg (2002). doi:10.1007/3-540-45876-X_30
16. Papenbrock, T., Bergmann, T., Finke, M., Zwiener, J., Naumann, F.: Data profiling with metanome. PVLDB **8**(12), 1860–1863 (2015)
17. Snodgrass, R.T.: The temporal query language TQUEL. ACM Trans. Database Syst. **12**(2), 247–298 (1987)

Design of Distributed Calculation Scheme Using Network Address Translation for Ad-hoc Wireless Positioning Network

Jumpei Kajimura[1], Shigemi Ishida[1]([✉]), Shigeaki Tagashira[2], and Akira Fukuda[1]

[1] ISEE, Kyushu University, Motooka 744, Nishi-ku, Fukuoka-shi, Fukuoka 819-0395, Japan
ishida@f.ait.kyushu-u.ac.jp
[2] Faculty of Informatics, Kansai University, Ryozenji-cho 2-1-1, Takatsuki-shi, Osaka 569-1095, Japan

Abstract. We have developed an ad-hoc wireless positioning network (AWPN) to realize on-demand indoor location-based services [10]. This paper extends our AWPN to handle huge number of localization requests. In AWPN, WiFi APs measure received signal strength (RSS) of WiFi signals and send the RSS information to a localization server via a WiFi mesh network. The maximum number of WiFi devices is therefore limited by computational resources on the localization server. We push this limit by introducing a new distributed calculation scheme: we use the MapReduce computation framework and perform map processes on APs and reduce processes on localization servers. We also utilize a network router capable of network address translation (NAT) for shuffle processes to provide scalability. We implemented and evaluated our distributed calculation scheme to demonstrate that our scheme almost evenly distributes localization calculations to multiple localization servers with approximately 26% variations.

Keywords: Ad-hoc wireless positioning network (AWPN) · MapReduce · Distributed calculation · Network address translation (NAT)

1 Introduction

In recent years, smartphones have become prevalent, which pushes increasing attention to location-based services. Location-based services are mainly developed for outdoor use because the global positioning system (GPS) is widely available in outdoor environments. Indoor localization is now more required to extend location-based services to indoor environments.

We are developing a WiFi ad-hoc wireless positioning network (AWPN) to realize on-demand indoor location-based services that are used in one-time use scenarios such as a navigation in an exhibition event. The AWPN is a localization system built on a WiFi mesh network. In AWPN, WiFi access points (APs)

© Springer International Publishing AG 2017
D. Kotzinos et al. (Eds.): ISIP 2016, CCIS 760, pp. 33–48, 2017.
DOI: 10.1007/978-3-319-68282-2_3

capture IEEE 802.11 `ProbeRequest` frames sent from a WiFi device and measure received signal strength (RSS) of the frames. The RSS-data is then sent to a localization server via a WiFi mesh network to estimate the device location.

When we use AWPN in a large indoor environment, the localization server receives huge number of RSS-data, which increases computational requirements on the localization server. Large-scale AWPN consists of many WiFi APs that receive signals from many WiFi devices. Although single localization calculation completes in few milliseconds [10], localization calculations for hundreds of WiFi devices require considerable time. Especially, smartphones send many `ProbeRequest` frames every second, which drastically increases the number of localization calculations.

To address the calculation load problem, the MapReduce distributed calculation systems [2,3] such as Hadoop [21] have been widely adopted. MapReduce systems, however, are inefficient for AWPN localization calculations because computational resource for distribution is not negligible. MapReduce systems consists of three processes: *map* process in which calculation tasks are associated with specific hash values named keys, *shuffle* process in which map tasks are distributed to calculation nodes based on the keys, and *reduce* process in which mapped data are aggregated to calculate final results. The MapReduce effectively distributes calculation load onto calculation nodes when the map and reduce processes are heavier than the shuffle process. In AWPN, localization calculation itself is lightweight computation. Shuffle processes and data communications between calculation nodes for shuffling are not negligible in AWPN.

As a new solution for the calculation load problem in AWPN, this paper presents a distributed calculation scheme such that MapReduce processes are distributed to APs and localization servers. In the proposed calculation scheme, APs perform map processes and localization servers perform reduce processes. The APs measure the RSS of a `ProbeRequest` frame and determine the localization server to send the RSS-data based on the information in the `ProbeRequest` frame. RSS-data, generated on multiple APs, of an identical `ProbeRequest` frame is therefore collected on the same localization server.

Practically, we utilize a network router for shuffle processes to easily support scalability. The required number of localization servers is dependent on the scale of AWPN and the number of WiFi devices to be localized. To avoid reconfiguration of WiFi APs in the environment when the number of localization servers changes, we use network address translation (NAT) on a network router to forward RSS-data to localization servers. The router is specified as a default gateway in AWPN to collect all the RSS-data on the router. RSS-data is forwarded to a specific localization server based on a key value in the RSS-data. The number change of localization servers only requires reconfiguration of address translation rules, which is defined in the network router.

Note that our approach is another form of MapReduce implementation with a simple feature set. Our distributed calculation scheme does not provide features such as dynamic scaling and fault tolerance that are widely available in original MapReduce systems. These features are often insignificant in localization systems for location-based services.

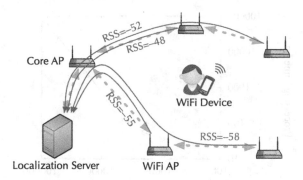

Fig. 1. Overview of ad-hoc wireless positioning network (AWPN)

To demonstrate the effectiveness of the proposed distributed calculation scheme, we conducted experimental evaluations in a Kyushu University building. The experimental evaluations reveal that the proposed distributed calculation scheme successfully distributed RSS-data to localization servers with imbalance of 26%.

The remainder of this paper is structured as follows. Section 2 briefly describes AWPN and shows requirements of a distributed calculation scheme in AWPN. In Sect. 3, we present a distributed calculation scheme using network address translation for AWPN, followed by implementation in Sect. 4. In Sect. 5, we conducted experimental evaluations of the proposed distributed calculation scheme. Finally, Sect. 6 concludes the paper.

2 Distributed Calculation in Ad-hoc Wireless Positioning Network

2.1 Ad-hoc Wireless Positioning Network

Ad-hoc Wireless Positioning Network (AWPN) is a WiFi mesh network capable of localizing WiFi devices [17]. Figure 1 depicts an overview of AWPN. To construct AWPN, we install multiple WiFi APs into a localization target area and connect a localization server to an AP named a core AP. The network is automatically constructed with multi-hop links between APs. APs detect a WiFi signal sent from a WiFi device in the localization target area and measures received signal strength (RSS) of the signal. The RSS-data and the WiFi device address are then sent to a localization server. The localization server calculates the device location using multilateration with the RSS-data sent from multiple APs.

In AWPN, calculation load becomes heavier as the number of RSS-data increases because the localization server performs all the calculations. Distributed calculation is an effective solution to address this calculation load problem.

There are two requirements for distributed calculation in AWPN.

The first requirement is independence between AWPN scale and system configurations. When we extend a localization target area, we need to add APs and

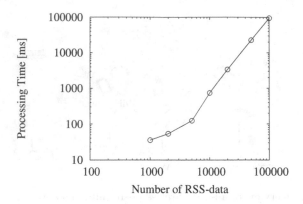

Fig. 2. RSS-data processing time on MongoDB

localization servers to process increased number of RSS-data. Changing system configurations such as AP configuration parameters, AP firmware, and localization server program requires much cost because there are hundreds of APs and localizations servers in AWPN.

The second requirement is small overhead. In large-scale AWPN, localization servers perform huge number of localization calculations because many WiFi devices transmit `ProbeRequest` frames more than once per second. Localization calculation is not a heavy task and is finished in few milliseconds [10]. Overhead for calculations including RSS-data reception should be minimized.

Figure 2 shows the time required for RSS-data processing on MongoDB distributed database [18]. We collected RSS-data using AWPN installed in our laboratory and inserted the RSS-data into MongoDB. On MongoDB, we grouped RSS-data by sender WiFi devices and counted the number of RSS-data in each group. We repeated data processing for 100 times and averaged the processing time. Figure 2 indicates that the processing time greatly increased as the number of RSS-data increased when the number of RSS-data was more than 5,000. We only counted the number of RSS-data in this example. We can confirm that overhead to retrieve data from database is considerable when we process huge number of RSS-data.

2.2   Related Works

For many high computation applications, MapReduce-based distributed calculation systems [2,3] are widely adopted to process high volume of data. For example, the MapReduce systems are utilized in machine learning as well as data mining [8,9,15], clustering [22], pairwise document similarity calculation [6], and genome analysis [16]. Also there are many MapReduce extensions such as MRPGA [13], Twister [4], DELMA [7], Tiled-MapReduce [1], SpatialHadoop [5], and epiC [12].

The MapReduce systems, however, suffer from high overhead for localization calculation in AWPN because localization calculation is a lightweight computational task. In the MapReduce systems, RSS-data is first stored in a distributed database. RSS-data is then analyzed and grouped by sender devices in map processes to calculate device location. In reduce processes, device location is calculated using the grouped RSS-data. A node called a master node distributes map and reduce processes to calculation nodes. In AWPN, the load of the master node becomes significant when processing huge number of RSS-data. Data reading from the distributed database in map and reduce processes is another overhead in AWPN because results of map and reduce processes are stored in distributed nodes.

Kafka [14] is a distributed messaging system for realtime data processing, which is another form of distributed calculation systems. In Kafka, producers generate messages and send the messages to servers named brokers, which provide distributed data queues. Application servers, named consumers, retrieve messages from brokers at their own rate to process the messages. When we apply Kafka to AWPN localization calculations, APs send RSS-data to brokers and localization servers consume the RSS-data. Using a gateway service, Kafka easily adapts to the change of the number of localization servers. This publish/subscribe model is also used in several IoT middlewares such as DDS [19] and DPWS [11].

Although distributed data processing schemes using a publish/subscribe model can perform localization calculations with high flexibility, a broker requires higher computational resources compared to our approach. Data storage on a broker is also required to safely process stream data. Our approach only requires network routers with sufficient network capacity.

3   Distributed Calculation Scheme for AWPN

3.1   Overview

Figure 3 shows an overview of our distributed calculation scheme using address translation. Our key idea is to distribute MapReduce processes to APs, network router, and localization servers. An AP receives a `ProbeRequest` frame and measures received signal strength (RSS) of the frame. The AP performs a map process; the AP calculates a key value based on the information in the `ProbeRequest` frame. The RSS value as well as key value is sent to a network router as RSS-data. When the network router receives RSS-data, the router performs a shuffle process; RSS-data is sent to the localization server associated with the key value in the RSS-data. The RSS-data with the same key values is therefore collected to the same localization server. The localization server then performs a reduce process, i.e., calculates location of a WiFi device.

Following subsections describe details of map and shuffle processes.

3.2   Map Process

In a map process, an AP calculates a key value based on the information in a `ProbeRequest` frame sent from a WiFi device. An AP retrieves the information below to calculate a key value:

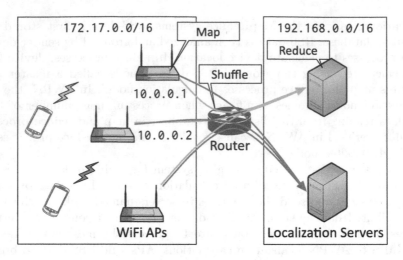

Fig. 3. Overview of distributed calculation scheme using network address translation for AWPN

– The MAC address of a source WiFi device
– The `sequence` number of a `ProbeRequest` frame
– The reception time of a `ProbeRequest` frame

The key values are associated with IP addresses in an address space not used in a WiFi mesh network. An AP sends RSS-data to the IP address associated with a calculated key value. We configure the WiFi mesh network to use a network router as a default gateway. All the RSS-data is therefore sent to the network router. In Fig. 3, for example, RSS-data sent to an address in 10.0.0.0/24 address space is actually sent to the network router because 10.0.0.0/24 is outside of 172.17.0.0/16 network.

Key value calculation algorithm should be simple enough because APs have limited computational resources. As a simple example in this paper, a key value k is calculated from the last byte m of the MAC address of a source WiFi device and the `sequence` number s of a `ProbeRequest` frame as

$$k = (m + s) \mod 256. \tag{1}$$

`Sequence` number should be included in a key calculation because a WiFi device successively sends `ProbeRequest` frames with different `sequence` numbers in a short time. For binding between key values and IP addresses, we map an 8-bit key value to a last byte of an IP address in 10.0.0.0/24 address space.

3.3 Shuffle Process

In a shuffle process, a network router changes the destination address of RSS-data using network address translation (NAT) to forward RSS-data to localization servers. The network router is responsible for distribution of RSS-data for

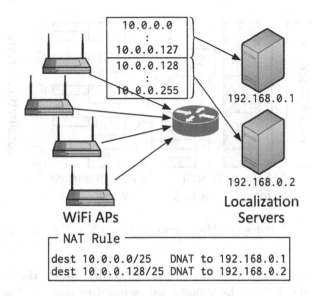

Fig. 4. Overview of shuffle process in network router

localization calculation. The number change of localization servers only requires reconfiguration of the network router.

Figure 4 shows an overview of a shuffle process in a network router. The figure shows an example with two localization servers 192.168.0.1 and 192.168.0.2. APs send RSS-data to an IP address in 10.0.0.0/24 address space. The destination address space 10.0.0.0/24 is divided into 10.0.0.0/25 and 10.0.0.128/25 subnets, each of which is assigned to a localization server. The network router performs network address translation with rules shown in Fig. 4 to forward RSS-data to localization servers. Although we can divide the destination address space at any point, the size of subnets should be the same to evenly distribute RSS-data to localization servers.

When the number N of localization servers is not the power of 2, i.e., $N \neq 2^n$ (n is zero or a positive integer), we need complicated address translation rules. For example, when we add another localization server in Fig. 4, we want to evenly divide the address space into three subnets below:

- 10.0.0.0 $\sim$ 10.0.0.84,
- 10.0.0.85 $\sim$ 10.0.0.169,
- 10.0.0.170 $\sim$ 10.0.0.255.

The size of a subnet is 85 or 86 in this case. Subnets are defined by a netmask, which restricts the size of a subnet to the power of 2. We cannot evenly divide the address space into three subnets with any netmask.

When $N \neq 2^n$, we divide an address space into subnets until the number of the subnets is greater than N and assign the subnets to localization servers. Here we explain the address division using an example when the number N of

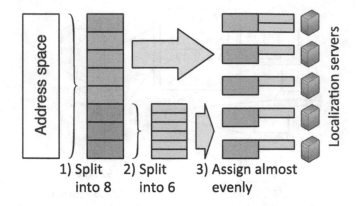

Fig. 5. Example of address space division ($N = 5$, $k_{max} = 2$)

localization servers is five as shown in Fig. 5. We first divide the address space into eight subnets. Five of the subnets are assigned to each localization server. Three remaining subnets are more divided into six small subnets, five of which are assigned to localization servers. We repeat this division process for up to k_{max} times and assign remaining subnets to localization servers as shown in Fig. 5.

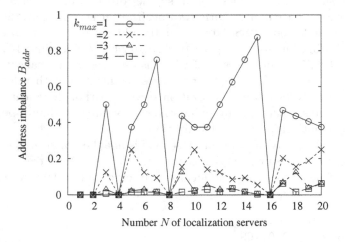

Fig. 6. Address imbalance B_{addr} as a function of the number N of localization servers ($k_{max} = 1, 2, 3, 4$)

Although the address division process results in imbalance of the number of addresses in subnets, the imbalance decreases as the maximum number k_{max} of divisions increases. Figure 6 shows address imbalance B_{addr} as a function of the number N of localization servers. Address imbalance B_{addr} is defined as

$$B_{addr} = \max \left| \frac{a_i - \bar{a}}{\bar{a}} \right|, \tag{2}$$

where a_i is the number of addresses assigned to localization server i and $\bar{a}$ is the average number of addresses assigned to localization servers. Address imbalance B_{addr} becomes 0 for an ideal case, i.e., addresses are evenly assigned to localization servers. Figure 6 indicates that the maximum address imbalance decreases as 0.875, 0.25, 0.125, and 0.063 as the maximum number k_{max} of divisions increases from 1 to 4. Increase in k_{max} results in increase in the computation load on a network router. k_{max} is determined based on computational resources on the router.

4 Implementation

We implemented the proposed distributed calculation scheme using off-the-shelf devices. Figure 7 shows the overview of our implementation. We installed four PicoCELA PCWL-0100 APs and a Netgear WNDR4300 network router, which are shown in Fig. 8. Table 1 shows specifications of PCWL. PCWLs are WiFi APs that automatically build a WiFi mesh network. We implemented a C program that captures `ProbeRequest` frames to generate RSS-data and perform map processes on Linux running on PCWL.

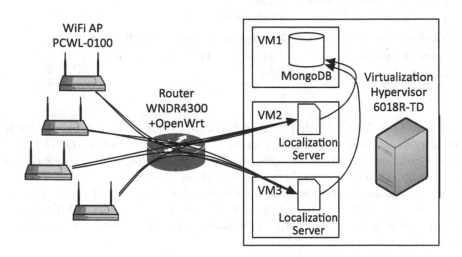

Fig. 7. Overview of implementation

We prepared three virtual machines: two for localization servers and one for a database server. The virtual machines were managed by the VMware ESXi 6.0 hypervisor running on a Supermicro 6018R-TD server with a 1.8 GHz eight-core

Fig. 8. AP and network router used in implementation

Table 1. Specifications of PCWL-0100 [20]

Range in line-of-sight	Approx. 150 m
TX power of mesh wireless	16 dBm
TX power of access wireless	16 dBm
Access wireless standard	IEEE 802.11b/g
Number of mesh wireless IFs	2 (except an access wireless IF) 5.15 ∼ 5.35 GHz
Physical dimensions	W142 mm × H118 mm × D39 mm
Weight	450 g

Intel XeonE5-2630Lv3 CPU, 16 GB memory, and four 2 TB disk drives. Each virtual machine used single CPU core and 2 GB memory. Debian/GNU Linux 8.0 was running on virtual machines, which were built on separate disk drives to minimize mutual influence between the virtual machines.

The localization server was implemented as a C++ program. The localization server received RSS-data from the network router and estimate WiFi device location using a simple multilateration algorithm. The results were sent to a MongoDB database server.

5   Evaluation

To validate the effectiveness of the proposed distributed calculation scheme presented in Sect. 3, we evaluated RSS-data imbalance that indicates fairness of

RSS-data distribution. We also evaluated the CPU usage and time for localization calculations as a function of RSS-data traffic to estimate the number of localization servers required for practical deployment.

In our evaluations, we used RSS-data collected in a real environment. We installed four PCWLs in our laboratory and collected RSS-data generated from `ProbeRequest` frames sent from user devices such as smartphones and laptops. The RSS-data was collected for approximately three and half days. The number of collected RSS-data is 137,061.

5.1 RSS-Data Imbalance

RSS-data imbalance is a figure that indicates how uniformly RSS-data is distributed to localization servers. RSS-data imbalance B_{rss} is defined in the same manner as the address imbalance as

$$B_{rss} = \max \left| \frac{r_i - \bar{r}}{\bar{r}} \right|, \tag{3}$$

where r_i is the number of RSS-data received on localization server i and $\bar{r}$ is the average number of RSS-data received on localization servers. RSS-data imbalance B_{rss} becomes 0 for an ideal case, i.e., RSS-data is evenly distributed to localization servers.

We calculated the number of RSS-data received on each localization server using the RSS-data collected in a real environment, while changing the number of localization servers. For each RSS-data, destination localization server was calculated using the map process described in Eq. (1) and the shuffle process presented in Sect. 3.3. RSS-data imbalance was calculated using Eq. (3) with the number of RSS-data received on each localization server.

Figure 9 shows RSS-data imbalance B_{rss} as a function of the number N of localization servers. Figure 9 indicates the following:

- Comparing Figs. 6 and 9, RSS-data imbalance B_{rss} curve is similar to the address imbalance curve in Fig. 6. When address imbalance was big, RSS-data was not evenly distributed to localization servers, resulting in big RSS-data imbalance.
- RSS-data imbalance B_{rss} had a tendency to decrease as the maximum number k_{max} of divisions increases. In a range of k_{max} from 1 to 4, RSS-data imbalance B_{rss} became maximum at 0.26 when $k_{max} = 3$.

From the above results, we conclude that a hash function used in a map process is a key factor to evenly distribute RSS-data in our distributed calculation scheme. The simple hash function presented in Eq. (1) in Sect. 3.2 exhibited low performance in terms of fair distribution of RSS-data.

5.2 CPU Usage

To validate that a localization calculation is not a heavy task compared to RSS-data reception, we evaluated CPU usage while changing RSS-data traffic, i.e., the

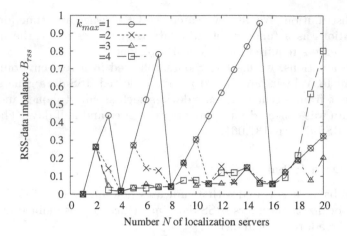

Fig. 9. RSS-data imbalance B_{rss} as a function of the number N of localization servers ($k_{max} = 1, 2, 3, 4$)

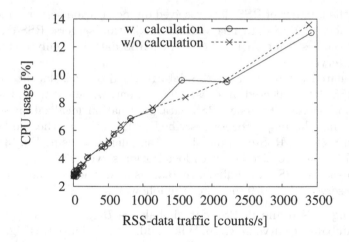

Fig. 10. CPU usage as a function of RSS-data traffic

number of RSS-data sent in one second. We sent dummy RSS-data at a specific rate and recorded average CPU usage for 300 s using `sysstat` command. Not to perform wasting calculations, we only sent RSS-data that can be successfully localized. We compared CPU usages with and without localization calculations.

Figure 10 shows CPU usage as a function of RSS-data traffic. Figure 10 indicates the following:

– CPU usage almost linearly increased as the RSS-data traffic increased. The numbers of RSS-data receptions and localization calculations are proportional to RSS-data traffic, which linearly increased CPU usage.

- There was a slight difference of CPU usages between with and without localization calculations. The difference of CPU usages between with and without
  localization calculations, i.e., CPU usage for localization calculations, was
  quite small.

The above results reveal that localization calculation is a lightweight task in
comparison with RSS-data reception.

5.3 Calculation Time

To estimate how many servers are required to localize huge number of WiFi
devices, we evaluated localization calculation time. We modified localization calculation program on a localization server installed in a real environment to record
start and end time for every localization calculation. Localization calculations
were performed for 80,941 times with 137,061 RSS-data.

Figure 11 shows an empirical cumulative distributed function (ECDF) of
localization calculation time. Black and blue lines in the Fig. 11 show the results
for all calculations and successful calculations, respectively. Figure 11 shows the
following:

- More than 80% of calculations were completed in 5 ms. Localization calculation is not a heavy task for a localization server and doesn't take much time
  for a single calculation.
- 83.6% of successful calculations were completed in 5 ms. 83.6% and 96.9% of
  successful calculations were completed in 5 and 10 ms, respectively. For more
  than 100 localization calculations per second, multiple servers or multi-thread
  programming is required to complete localizations in realtime.

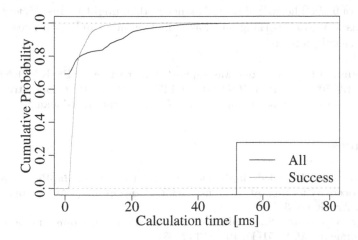

Fig. 11. Empirical cumulative distributed function (ECDF) of localization calculation
time for all and successful calculations (Color figure online)

6,955 localization calculations have been succeeded, which is 8.6% of all the calculations. We used four APs in this evaluation and calculated device location using multilateration. Multilateration requires RSS-data from all the four APs to estimate device location in our evaluation environment. 69.3% of localization calculations failed because of less number of RSS-data, which completed in 5 ms. Remainder 22.1% of calculations diverged because of the variations of RSS caused by multi-paths and measurement errors, which took longer time.

The above results reveal that our distributed calculation scheme requires parallel computation for more than 100 localization calculations per second. Referring to Sect. 5.2, the number of localization servers might be estimated based on the CPU usage of RSS-data reception. As shown in Fig. 10, the CPU usage linearly increases as RSS-data traffic increases. We might need more than two servers when RSS-data traffic is more than 25,000 counts every second. The RSS-data traffic greatly increases as the numbers of WiFi devices and APs increase.

6   Conclusion

This paper presented a new distributed calculation scheme for an ad-hoc wireless positioning network (AWPN) to process huge number of localization requests. Our approach is to distribute MapReduce processes to WiFi APs, a network router, and localization servers: map processes on APs, shuffle processes on a router, and reduce processes on localization servers. Using network address translation (NAT) in shuffle processes, our distributed calculation scheme easily provides scalability with variable number of localization servers. We conducted experimental evaluations in a real environment and confirmed that our scheme successfully distributed localization calculations with the maximum RSS-data imbalance of 0.26. The RSS-data imbalance of 0.26 might be insufficient in practical use cases. We are working on a hash function in a shuffling process to evenly distribute calculation tasks.

Acknowledgments. This work was supported in part by JSPS KAKENHI Grant Numbers 15H05708, 15K12021, 16K16048, and 17H01741, and the Cooperative Research Project of the Research Institute of Electrical Communication, Tohoku University.

References

1. Chen, R., Chen, H.: Tiled-MapReduce: efficient and flexible MapReduce processing on multicore with tiling. ACM Trans. Archit. Code Optim. (TACO) **10**(1), 3:1–3:30 (2013). Article no. 3
2. Dean, J., Ghemawat, S.: MapReduce: simplified data programming on large clusters. Commun. ACM **51**(1), 107–113 (2008)
3. Dean, J., Ghemawat, S.: MapReduce: a flexible data processing tool. Commun. ACM **53**(1), 72–77 (2010)

4. Ekanayake, J., Li, H., Zhang, B., Gunarathne, T., Bae, S.H.: Twister: a runtime for iterative MapReduce. In: Proceedings of the ACM International Symposium on High Performance Distributed Computing (HPDC), pp. 810–818, June 2010
5. Eldawy, A.: SpatialHadoop: towards flexible and scalable spatial processing using MapReduce. In: Proceedings of the ACM SIGMOD PhD Symposium, pp. 46–50, June 2014
6. Elsayed, T., Lin, J., Oard, D.W.: Pairwise document similarity in large collections with MapReduce. In: Proceedings of the ACL, Human Language Technologies: Short Papers (HLT-Short), pp. 265–268, June 2008
7. Fadika, Z., Govindaraju, M.: DELMA: dynamically ELastic MApReduce framework for CPU-intensive applications. In: Proceedings of IEEE/ACM International Symposium on Cluster, Cloud and Grid Computing (CCGrid), pp. 454–463, May 2011
8. Ghoting, A., Kambadur, P., Pednault, E., Kannan, R.: NIMBLE: a toolkit for the implementation of parallel data mining and machine learning algorithms on MapReduce. In: Proceedings of the ACM KDD, pp. 334–342, August 2011
9. Ghoting, A., Krishnamurthy, R., Pednault, E., Reinwald, B., Sindhwani, V., Tatikonda, S., Tian, Y., Vaithyanathan, S.: SystemML: declarative machine learning on MapReduce. In: Proceedings of IEEE International Conference on Data Engineering (ICDE), pp. 231–242, April 2011
10. Ishida, S., Tagashira, S., Arakawa, Y., Fukuda, A.: On-demand indoor location-based service using ad-hoc wireless positioning network. In: Proceedings of the IEEE International Conference on Embedded Software and Systems (ICESS), pp. 1005–1013, August 2015
11. Jammes, F., Mensch, A., Smit, H.: Service-oriented device communications using the devices profile for web services. In: Proceedings of the ACM International Workshop on Middleware for Pervasive and Ad-Hoc Computing (MPAC), November–December 2005
12. Jiang, D., Wu, S., Chen, G., Ooi, B.C., Tan, K.L., Ku, J.: epiC: an extensible and scalable system for processing big data. VLDB J. **25**(1), 3–26 (2016)
13. Jin, C., Vecchiola, C., Buyya, R.: MRPGA: an extention of MapReduce for parallelizing genetic algorithms. In: Proceedings of the IEEE International Conference on eScience, pp. 214–221, December 2008
14. Kreps, J., Narkhede, N., Rao, J.: Kafka: a distributed messaging system for log processing. In: Proceedings of the International Workshop on Networking Meets Databases (NetDB), pp. 1–7, June 2011
15. Low, Y., Bickson, D., Gonzalez, J., Guestrin, C., Kyrola, A., Hellerstein, J.M.: Distributed GraphLab: a framework for machine learning and data mining in the cloud. In: Proceedings of the International Conference on Very Large Scale Data Bases (VLDB), pp. 716–727, August 2012
16. McKenna, A., Hanna, M., Banks, E., Sivachenko, A., Cibulskis, K., Kernytsky, A., Garimella, K., Altshuler, D., Gabriel, S., Daly, M., DePristo, M.A.: The genome analysis toolkit: a MapReduce framework for analyzing next-generation DNA sequencing data. Genome Res. **20**(9), 1297–1303 (2010)
17. Miwa, N., Tagashira, S., Matsuda, H., Tsutsui, T., Arakawa, Y., Fukuda, A.: A multilateration-based localization scheme for adhoc wireless positioning networks used in information-oriented construction. In: Proceedings of the IEEE International Conference on Advanced Information Networking and Applications (AINA), pp. 690–695, March 2013
18. MongoDB Inc.: MongoDB. https://www.mongodb.com/

19. Object Management Group: The OMG data-distribution service for real-time systems (DDS). http://portals.omg.org/dds/
20. PicoCELA: PCWL-0100 catalog. http://www.picocela.com/
21. The Apache Software Foundation: Apache Hadoop. http://hadoop.apache.org/
22. Zhao, W., Ma, H., He, Q.: Parallel K-means clustering based on MapReduce. In: Jaatun, M.G., Zhao, G., Rong, C. (eds.) CloudCom 2009. LNCS, vol. 5931, pp. 674–679. Springer, Heidelberg (2009). doi:10.1007/978-3-642-10665-1_71

Mobility Data Analysis

Latent Variable Model for Weather-Aware Traffic State Analysis

Akira Kinoshita[1,2]([envelope]), Atsuhiro Takasu[2], and Jun Adachi[2]

[1] The University of Tokyo, 7-3-1 Hongo, Bunkyo, Tokyo, Japan
[2] National Institute of Informatics, 2-1-2 Hitotsubashi, Chiyoda, Tokyo, Japan
{kinoshita,takasu,adachi}@nii.ac.jp

Abstract. Because vehicular traffic is affected by weather conditions, knowledge of the relationship between weather and traffic enables attempts to improve social services through applications such as situation-aware anomaly vehicle detection and snow-removal planning in snowy countries. We propose a *weather-aware traffic state model* for vehicular traffic analysis in consideration of weather conditions. The model is a probabilistic latent variable model that integrates weather and traffic data, whereby the characteristics of the traffic according to location, time, and weather condition are obtained automatically. After we observe both weather and travel times along road segments, we derive the expectation–maximization algorithm for model parameter estimation and the predictive distribution of travel time given the weather observation values. We evaluated the model qualitatively and quantitatively using winter traffic and weather data for the city of Sapporo, Japan, which is a large city that suffers heavy snowfalls. The empirical analysis with model visualization outcomes demonstrated the relationship between the expected vehicular speed and weather conditions, and showed the potential bottleneck segments for given weather conditions. The quantitative evaluation showed that our model fits the data better than a linear regression model, which suggests the potential for anomaly detection from vehicular observation data.

Keywords: Data integration · Data mining · Latent variable models · Probe-car data · Social cyber–physical systems · Weather-aware traffic state analysis

1 Introduction

Real-world traffic is complex and involves various factors. One important factor is the weather conditions. These change the driving environment, including visibility and road surface conditions, which affects the movement of vehicles in terms of running speed, vehicular gaps, and so on. Bad weather also affects the behavior of people: they may change their destination or visiting order, or avoid traveling at all, which affects the traffic volume and travel route. Knowledge of the relationship between weather and traffic enables attempts to improve social services.

© Springer International Publishing AG 2017
D. Kotzinos et al. (Eds.): ISIP 2016, CCIS 760, pp. 51–65, 2017.
DOI: 10.1007/978-3-319-68282-2_4

For example, if the roads and intersections in which heavy snow often hinders the traffic are known, effective road improvement and snow-removal planning will be available. Situation-aware detection of anomalies in vehicle movements will also be possible with such knowledge and the awareness of the current condition. This approach also promises to provide finer-grained traffic information than existing approaches: for instance, that traffic is congested because the average speed has fallen below a prescribed value.

The relationship between weather and vehicular traffic has been studied over decades. Traffic engineers studied the effect of weather on freeway traffic in 1988 [5]. Keay and Simmonds analyzed the relationship between rainfall and traffic volume in Melbourne, Australia, using a linear regression method [7]. Recent studies also utilized linear regression techniques but they are application-oriented. Lee et al. developed a linear regression model to predict traffic congestion using weather data [9]. Tanimura et al. also used a linear regression model to predict the reductions in vehicle speeds in snowy conditions [11]. Xu et al. predicted traffic flows based on weather data using an artificial neural network as well as a linear regression method [13]. These studies model the relationship between weather and traffic in terms of traffic statistics or aggregated values. However, they do not model the relationship between weather and the behavior of individual vehicles.

The movement of a vehicle differs substantially among individuals. In particular, on ordinary roads, the speeds of vehicles vary greatly because they frequently slow down for intersections, traffic lights, and pedestrians. Therefore, in this paper, we model the traffic by probabilistic means. With the probabilistic distribution of the traffic observation values, such as travel time at a certain location over a selected period, the degree of anomaly of the observed behavior of an individual vehicle can be evaluated quantitatively. Statistics such as mean travel time and average speed can also be calculated based on the distribution. Earlier studies proposed several probabilistic distribution models [2, 4, 14]; however, they have not considered the weather conditions.

In this paper, we develop a *weather-aware traffic state model* (WATS model), a probabilistic model of observed values for traffic with consideration of weather conditions. Our probabilistic model aims at learning the "normal" patterns of traffic using data archives, which would be used for the applications described above, i.e., traffic incident detection and snow-removal planning. We have previously proposed a latent variable model for traffic state, and have shown its effectiveness for incident detection on expressways [8]. This model introduced latent traffic states such as "smooth" and "congested," and assumed the traffic observation values depend on the latent states. This paper extends the model by introducing variables related to weather conditions and relationships among the variables. The WATS model assumes not only that the traffic observation value depends on latent traffic states, but also that the traffic state depends on the weather. We introduce weather states to relate the traffic data to the weather data observed at the same time of day, thus allowing the relationship between weather and traffic to be learned. We borrow the idea of a Pachinko allocation model [10], which is a latent variable model that analyzes topics in textual information by considering correlations among latent information, to realize a feasible model for the problem.

We also aim to apply the WATS model to ordinary roads as well as expressways. In this study, we conducted an experiment in the city of Sapporo, Hokkaido, Japan. Sapporo is the metropolis of Hokkaido prefecture, and the fourth largest city in Japan in terms of population. While more than 1.9 M people live there, the city is located in a heavy snowfall region. The city spent more than 18 billion yen (about \$US 150 M) on plans to counter snow in the 2015 fiscal year, with more than three quarters of the budget devoted to snow removal [3]. It is important to enhance cost effectiveness while reducing the bad influence of snow on traffic. Against this background, we attempted an empirical analysis on the weather–traffic relationship in Sapporo in winter. The visualized results of the WATS model indicate that it is possible to find bottlenecks that change according to weather and time. Our quantitative evaluation showed that the model fits the data better than an existing weather–traffic model, suggesting the potential for incident detection.

The main contributions of this paper are as follows.

- We propose a *weather-aware traffic state* (WATS) *model*. It is a new probabilistic latent variable model that integrates weather and traffic data, deriving the characteristics of the traffic according to location, time, and weather condition automatically.
- We show the effectiveness and the potential of the WATS model by our empirical qualitative and quantitative evaluations. The evaluation was conducted in the city of Sapporo, located in Japan's snow country.

The rest of this paper is organized as follows. In Sect. 2, we propose the WATS model. Section 3 reports the result of our empirical experiment and discusses the results, issues and future work. Finally, Sect. 4 concludes the paper.

2   Weather-Aware Traffic State Model

In this section, we present our WATS model. The aim of our model is to integrate observation data, traffic conditions, and weather conditions, so that the relationship between weather and vehicular traffic can be analyzed. Table 1 summarizes the notation used in this paper.

2.1   Model Design Concepts

We use two kinds of data:

- weather observation data, which are obtained periodically (e.g., hourly),
- traffic observation data, which are obtained intermittently or continuously.

Table 1. Notation

Notation	Definition
s	Road segment
d_s	Length of road segment s
S	Number of road segments
t	Time
T	Number of weather observation data
n	Index of traffic observation data
N_{ts}	Number of traffic observation data in segment s in time t
w	Weather observation data
D	Dimension of w
x	Traffic observation data
μ, Λ	Mean and precision, respectively, of w
λ	Mean travel speed
l, k	Index of latent states
L, K	Number of latent weather and traffic states, respectively
π	Mixing coefficient of weather states
v	Latent weather state
y, z	Latent weather and traffic state, respectively
θ	Mixing coefficient of traffic states
Θ	Set of parameters: $(\pi, \theta, \mu, \Lambda, \lambda)$
η	All hyperparameters: $(\alpha, \beta, a, b, \mu_0, \gamma, W, \nu)$

Here we develop a latent variable model, whereby weather-aware traffic performance is described in terms of a probability distribution.

Weather observation data indicate the weather conditions in the subject area. At time t, only one weather observation data point w is obtained. The observation value is numerical and we assume w follows a Gaussian distribution with mean μ and precision (i.e., the inverse of the covariance matrix) Λ. The mean and covariance can change according to weather conditions. For example, temperature tends to be low and snowfall tends to be large in "snowy" conditions, and temperature tends to be high and snowfall tends to be zero in "sunny" conditions. We introduce L weather states, each of which is characterized by the mean μ_l and the precision Λ_l. Then the probability distribution of the weather observation at time t is described in terms of a mixture of these components:

$$p(w_t \mid \Theta) = \sum_{l=1}^{L} \pi_{tl} \mathcal{N}(w_t \mid \mu_t \mid \Lambda_l^{-1}), \qquad (1)$$

where π_t is the mixing coefficient vector at time t. π_{tl} is equivalent to the probability of being in the l-th weather state at time t. The mixing coefficient varies according to the time t while each of L component Gaussians is identical over time. Therefore, π_t characterizes the weather condition at time t.

Intuitively, we can identify traffic states as being "smooth" or "congested," regardless of location, and the traffic state information is strongly related to geographical and time-of-day conditions [8]. Therefore, traffic observations are conducted for each *segment* s, which is the unit for traffic observation and is specified by road segment, direction, and time period, such as "morning" or "evening." At time t, N_{ts} traffic observation data points are obtained from segment s.

There are several options for traffic observation values, e.g., travel time and average speed. In this paper, we use travel time as the traffic observation value x. Travel time can be measured directly using probe cars [12]. The travel time depends on both the length of the road segment and traffic condition, and we model the relationship among them. Although several models have been proposed for travel time distribution [2,4], they are too complicated to incorporate into our model or they need additional features for estimation. Intuitively, traffic conditions can be characterized by the average speed λ: the traffic is "smooth" if λ is large, and "congested" if λ is small. We therefore introduce K traffic states with different average speeds $\{\lambda_k\}$ and the gamma distribution Gamma(d_s, λ_k), where d_s is the road length of the segment s. This distribution makes sense with the assumption of a Poisson process: considering the *event* that a vehicle goes forward a unit length, the rate λ, or average number of times the event occurs, is equivalent to the average speed, and the total time required for k occurrences of the event is equivalent to the travel time on a road of length k and follows an Erlang distribution. The gamma distribution is the generalized form of the Erlang distribution by allowing k to be a positive real number rather than a positive integer. Note that we use the notation Gamma(d_s, λ_k) in this paper for the gamma distribution with the following probability density function:

$$\text{Gamma}(x \mid d_s, \lambda_k) = \frac{\lambda_k^{d_s} x^{d_s-1}\exp(-\lambda_k x)}{\Gamma(d_s)}, \tag{2}$$

where $\Gamma(z)$ is the gamma function.

Traffic conditions vary according to the time and place and depend on the "condition" there, e.g., road shape and congestion occurrence. The condition can also change according to the weather even at a particular place. For example, traffic congestion may occur when it snows. There seems to be a hierarchical property: traffic observations depend on the traffic conditions, and the traffic conditions depend on the weather conditions. In this study, we model the relationship as a latent variable model, borrowing the idea of the Pachinko allocation model (PAM) [10]. PAM was proposed to analyze topics in textual information with consideration of correlations among latent information. It introduces a hierarchical structure among latent variables: word occurrence in a document depends on its topic and the topic depends on the supertopic. In our WATS model, the traffic observation value depends on the traffic state and the traffic state depends on the weather state. The probability distribution of the traffic

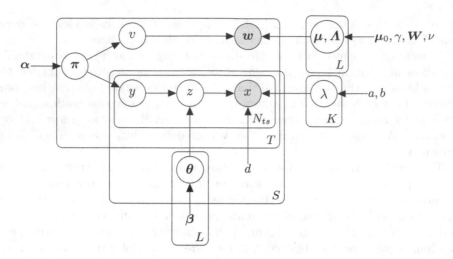

Fig. 1. Graphical model for the WATS model.

observation value is described in terms of a hierarchical mixture:

$$p(x_{tsn} \mid \Theta) = \sum_{l=1}^{L} \pi_{tl} \sum_{k=1}^{K} \theta_{slk} \mathrm{Gamma}(x_{tsn} \mid d_s, \lambda_k), \tag{3}$$

where θ_{sl} is the mixing coefficient vector, the k-th element of which is equivalent to the probability of being in the k-th traffic state in segment s in the l-th weather state. Each of K component gamma distributions is identical regardless of the segment and the weather state. Therefore, θ_{sl} characterizes the traffic performance for each road segment and for each weather state.

2.2   Generative Model

Figure 1 shows the graphical model for the WATS model. The upper part generates the weather observation data w_t while the lower part generates the traffic observation data x_{tsn}. The two kinds of data in the same time t are associated with each other by the parameter π_t. The generative process is as follows:

1. Generate parameters:
   (a) Generate the mean speed $\lambda_k \sim \mathrm{Gamma}(a, b)$ for each of K traffic states;
   (b) Generate the pair of the mean vector and the precision matrix of the weather observation values $(\mu_l, \Lambda_l) \sim \mathrm{Gauss\text{--}Wishart}(\mu_0, \gamma, W, \nu)$ for each of L weather states;
   (c) Generate the mixing coefficient $\theta_{sl} \sim \mathrm{Dirichlet}(\beta_l)$ for each segment s and for each weather state l;
2. Generate the data at time t:
   (a) Generate a mixing coefficient $\pi_t \sim \mathrm{Dirichlet}(\alpha)$;
   (b) Generate weather observation data:

    i. Generate the weather state $v_t \sim \text{Multinomial}(\boldsymbol{\pi}_t)$;

    ii. Generate the weather observation vector $\boldsymbol{w}_t \sim \mathcal{N}(\boldsymbol{\mu}_l, \boldsymbol{\Lambda}_l^{-1})$, where $v_t = l$.

(c) Generate the nth traffic observation data for each segment s:

    i. Generate $y_{tsn} \sim \text{Multinomial}(\boldsymbol{\pi}_t)$;

    ii. Generate $z_{tsn} \sim \text{Multinomial}(\boldsymbol{\theta}_{sl})$, where $y_{tsn} = l$;

    iii. Generate $x[tsn] \sim \text{Gamma}(d_s, \lambda_k)$, where $z_{tsn} = k$.

According to the generative process above, the log-likelihood is derived as follows:

$$\sum_t \ln \sum_l \pi_{tl} \mathcal{N}(\boldsymbol{w}_t \mid \boldsymbol{\mu}_l, \boldsymbol{\Lambda}_l^{-1}) + \sum_{t,s,n} \ln \sum_{l,k} \pi_{tl} \theta_{slk} \text{Gamma}(x_{tsn} \mid d_s, \lambda_k). \quad (4)$$

2.3 Model Estimation

Maximum-likelihood (ML) estimations or maximum a posteriori (MAP) estimations for latent variable models generally use the expectation–maximization (EM) algorithm [1]. The EM algorithm iterates E- and M-steps alternately until the log-likelihood converges. We show the update formulas for our WATS model; they can be derived by considering some conditional probabilities based on the graphical model, but the mathematical details of the derivation are are omitted here because of space limitations.

The E-step calculates the posteriors:

$$\zeta_{tl} \equiv p(v_t = l \mid \boldsymbol{w}_t, \boldsymbol{\Theta}) \qquad \propto \pi_{tl} \mathcal{N}(\boldsymbol{w}_t \mid \boldsymbol{\mu}_l, \boldsymbol{\Lambda}_l^{-1}), \quad (5)$$

$$\xi_{tsnlk} \equiv p(y_{tsn} = l, z_{tsn} = k \mid x_{tsn}, \boldsymbol{\Theta}) \propto \pi_{tl} \theta_{slk} \text{Gamma}(x_{tsn} \mid d_s, \lambda_k). \quad (6)$$

The M-step maximizes the following Q function for the ML estimation, or the $\tilde{Q}$ function for the MAP estimation:

$$Q = \sum_{t,l} \zeta_{tl} \left[\ln \mathcal{N}(\boldsymbol{w}_t \mid \boldsymbol{\mu}_l, \boldsymbol{\Lambda}_l^{-1}) + \ln \pi_{tl} \right]$$

$$+ \sum_{t,s,n,l,k} \xi_{tsnlk} \left[\ln \text{Gamma}(x_{tsn} \mid d_s, \lambda_k) + \ln \theta_{slk} + \ln \pi_{tl} \right], \quad (7)$$

$$\tilde{Q} = Q + \ln p(\boldsymbol{\Theta}). \quad (8)$$

This Q or $\tilde{Q}$ is maximized by introducing Lagrange multipliers and setting its partial derivatives with respect to each parameter to zero. The update formulas for MAP estimation are derived as follows:

$$\pi_{tl} \propto \zeta_{tl} + \sum_{s,n,k} \xi_{tsnlk} + \alpha_l - 1, \quad \theta_{slk} \propto \sum_{t,n} \xi_{tsnlk} + \beta_{lk} - 1, \quad (9)$$

$$\lambda_k = \frac{\sum_{t,s,n,l} \xi_{tsnlk} d_s + a - 1}{\sum_{t,s,n,l} \xi_{tsnlk} x_{tsn} + b}, \quad \boldsymbol{\mu}_l = \frac{\sum_t \zeta_{tl} \boldsymbol{w}_t + \gamma \boldsymbol{\mu}_0}{\sum_t \zeta_{tl} + \gamma}, \quad (10)$$

$$\boldsymbol{\Lambda}_l^{-1} = \frac{\sum_t \zeta_{tl}(\boldsymbol{w}_t - \boldsymbol{\mu}_l)(\boldsymbol{w}_t - \boldsymbol{\mu}_l)^\mathsf{T} + \gamma(\boldsymbol{\mu}_l - \boldsymbol{\mu}_0)(\boldsymbol{\mu}_l - \boldsymbol{\mu}_0)^\mathsf{T} + \boldsymbol{W}^{-1}}{\sum_t \zeta_{tl} + \nu - D}. \quad (11)$$

π_{tl} and θ_{slk} should be normalized so that $\sum_l \pi_{tl} = 1$ and $\sum_k \theta_{slk} = 1$ respectively. As for the ML estimation, constant terms (i.e., terms that do not include ζ_{tl} or ξ_{tsnlk}) are simply eliminated.

2.4 Prediction

Once the model parameter Θ is estimated, we can calculate the predictive distribution of travel time x in the segment s as the conditional probability given a weather observation vector w. Based on the graphical model, the predictive distribution is derived as follows:

$$p(x \mid w, s, \Theta) = \sum_k \omega_k \text{Gamma}(x \mid d_s, \lambda_k), \qquad (12)$$

where

$$\omega_k \equiv \frac{\sum_l \theta_{slk} \alpha_l \left(q(w) + \mathcal{N}(w \mid \mu_l, \Lambda_l^{-1}) \right)}{\left(\sum_l \alpha_l + 1 \right) q(w)}, \qquad (13)$$

$$q(w) \equiv \sum_l \alpha_l \mathcal{N}(w \mid \mu_l, \Lambda_l^{-1}). \qquad (14)$$

Therefore, the predicted travel time follows a gamma mixture distribution. The expected travel time is obtained as follows:

$$\mathbb{E}[x \mid w, s, \Theta] = \sum_k \omega_k \frac{d_s}{\lambda_k}. \qquad (15)$$

The predictive distribution and the expected value above include the hyperparameter α in the formulas. It is given in the MAP estimation, but it is not given in the ML estimation. According to Eqs. (7) and (8), the ML estimation can be regarded as a MAP estimation that assumes that the prior $p(\Theta)$ is uniform, i.e., constant. α is the parameter of a Dirichlet distribution, which is equivalent to a uniform distribution when $\alpha = 1$, i.e., $\alpha_l = 1$ for all l. Therefore, we propose to use $\alpha = 1$ for prediction with the estimated value of ML estimation.

3 Experiment

We have conducted an empirical winter traffic analysis in the city of Sapporo by applying the WATS model to real weather and traffic data. This section reports and discusses the experimental results.

3.1 Data Set

Figure 2 shows the subject area, a part of Sapporo, Hokkaido, Japan. Snow falls in Sapporo from the end of October to April and the snow depth reaches about

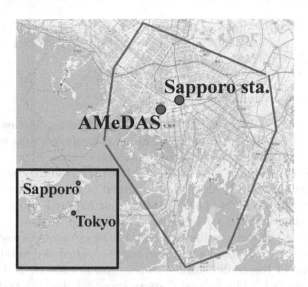

Fig. 2. Map of Sapporo, Hokkaido, Japan. The red-line polygon shows the subject area. The Sapporo AMeDAS station is also shown. Map tiles ©OpenStreetMap contributors, CC BY-SA 2.0.

one meter in midwinter every year. Surface weather such as temperature and precipitation is observed at about 1300 stations in Japan using the Automated Meteorological Data Acquisition System (AMeDAS) developed and operated by the Japan Meteorological Agency [6]. In this experiment, we used weather observation data from Sapporo AMeDAS station and traffic data within the region shown in Fig. 2; the nearest AMeDAS station is Sapporo.

We obtained probe-car data in Sapporo city, and then we preprocessed them to generate traffic data for each road segment. The original probe-car data include trajectory information, i.e., a sequence of time–location data points for each active probe car. The preprocess had five phases: we defined segments according to the road segments and time period; map matching was conducted to associate a vehicular location with a road segment; trajectory data were interpolated linearly so that the time when the vehicle entered or exited the segment was determined; and the travel time for each segment was observed. As mentioned previously, each *segment* was determined by road segment, direction, and time period. Our road segments follow the main road segment data in a commercial digital road map. They are divided by day (weekday or holiday) and by time period: morning rush hour (7–10 h), daytime (10–17 h), evening rush hour (17–20 h), and night (20–7 h on the following day). For the weather observation data, we used hourly data at Sapporo AMeDAS station, including temperature [°C], snowfall [cm/h], snow depth [cm], and precipitation [mm/h].

We obtained weather and traffic data from January 2010 to February 2015, but we used only winter data from October to April of each year. We used data in or before April 2014 for model training, and that in and after October 2014 for testing. We removed noisy segments that have less than 1000 training data points from the data set. The final training data include 31,891 segments and 74,826,640 traffic observations.

3.2   Parameter Estimation

We first trained the WATS model using the training data. In this experiment, we conducted ML estimation. We assumed eight weather states and 16 traffic states, but we did not assume any other parameter values such as mean speed or mean temperature, which were estimated from the training data.

We implemented the EM algorithm described in the previous section using OpenMP for multiprocessing. The EM algorithm required about 13 min using parallel processing with 36 CPU cores. Tables 2 and 3 show the estimated parameter values. The eight estimated weather states include snowy conditions ($l = 1, 2, 4$), warm conditions (7, 8), and snow-accumulated conditions (1–6). The mean speed of the traffic states extends over a wide range from "almost stopped" to "very fast." The estimated mean speed for the 16th traffic state was quite fast; this seems to be caused by outliers in the training data, which were possibly caused by map-matching failures. However, these would be insignificant in this experiment because the estimated mixing coefficient value for the 16th traffic state was zero or almost zero for almost all segments; that is, the 16th traffic state was ignored automatically.

We visualized the estimated model as shown in Fig. 3 for a qualitative analysis. Because of space limitations, the figure shows the estimated model only for the morning rush hour on weekdays. The color of a segment indicates the expected values of average link speeds; their probability densities were obtained

Table 2. Estimated mean parameters for each weather state distribution. The weather states are ordered by temperature.

Weather state l	1	2	3	4	5	6	7	8
Temperature [°C]	−3.6	−2.9	−2.4	−1.8	−1.4	1.1	8.3	8.8
Snowfall [cm/h]	2	1	0	3	0	0	0	0
Snow depth [cm]	65	56	66	47	56	17	0	0
Precipitation [mm/h]	1.1	0.5	0.0	2.4	0.6	0.0	1.4	0.0

Table 3. Estimated mean parameter for each traffic state distribution. The traffic states are ordered by mean speed.

Traffic state k	1	2	3	4	5	6	7	8
Mean speed [km/h]	1.2	3.0	5.0	7.2	10.0	13.4	17.6	23.3
Traffic state k	9	10	11	12	13	14	15	16
Mean speed [km/h]	31.0	39.4	48.1	56.9	65.6	75.4	96.7	295.5

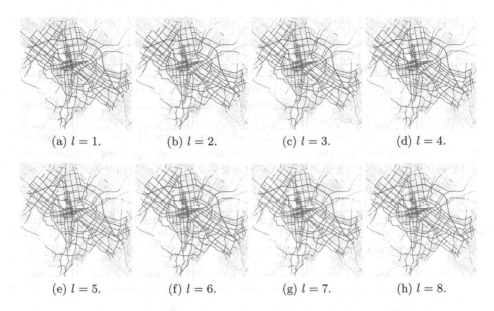

(a) $l = 1$.   (b) $l = 2$.   (c) $l = 3$.   (d) $l = 4$.

(e) $l = 5$.   (f) $l = 6$.   (g) $l = 7$.   (h) $l = 8$.

Fig. 3. Estimated model for the morning rush hour (7–10 h) on weekdays. The color of a segment indicates the expected value of the average link speed. Green represents high speed (100 km/h), red is moderate speed (50 km/h), and blue is "almost stopped" (0 km/h). Each subfigure corresponds to one of the eight weather states. Base map tiles ©OpenStreetMap contributors, Who's On First, and openstreetmapdata.com. Data are licensed under ODbL. (Color figure online)

by the transformation of random variables using the estimated travel time distribution and the road length. The map tends to be red as the weather states become warmer with less snow, but the map of the 6th state is exceptional because it is almost blue. This suggests that the traffic tends to slow down almost everywhere when the temperature is nearly zero degrees and there is snow accumulation. Vehicles can be expected to slow down in such weather conditions because the accumulated snow melts and freezes at around zero degrees and makes the road surface condition very poor. On the other hand, some road links keep the mean travel speed over different weather states at a slow value. We speculate that the reason is queueing and waiting for traffic lights regardless of weather.

3.3   Model Evaluation

We evaluated two quantitative metrics: prediction error of the expected travel time and the cross entropy. For comparison, we also trained linear regression models for each segment as the baseline.

Expected Travel Time Prediction. With the estimated model, we calculated the expected travel time for each road segment every hour. We used ML estimation in this experiment, so the expected value was given by Eq. (15) with $\alpha = 1$ as we described in the previous section. We regarded the sample mean of the actual travel times of vehicles in the test data as the ground truth in this experiment. Statistically, the number of samples should be large enough to be a reliable estimator of the ground truth. We therefore employed only the test cases that included 30 or more actual travel time observations per hour. We obtained 141 test cases from 68 segments.

Figure 4 shows the distribution of prediction error with the WATS model. Here it can be seen that the error distribution has a sharp peak around zero. The absolute prediction error was less than 2.5 s for more than 40% of the test cases and less than 20 s for 90%.

Figure 5 shows the comparison of the prediction error between the WATS model and the linear regression method. For this evaluation, the linear regression model was trained for each segment using the training data, with the hourly weather observation value w being the input value and with the mean travel

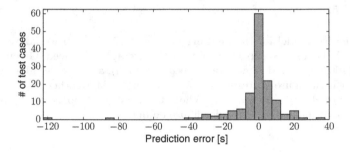

Fig. 4. Histogram of prediction errors for expected travel time calculated with the WATS model. Positive error means that the predicted travel time was longer than the ground truth, and vice versa.

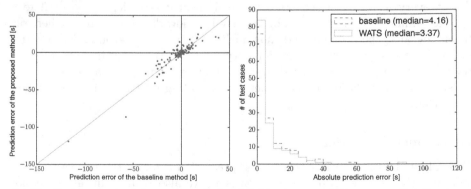

(a) Prediction error of the two methods. (b) Absolute prediction error distribution.

Fig. 5. Comparison of the prediction performance of the expected travel time between the linear regression (baseline) method and the proposed (WATS) model.

time per hour being the target value. In the left figure, each point corresponds to a test case, and the error of the proposed method against the baseline method is shown. The plots are substantially along the identity line shown as a red line, and there are both improved and worse cases. The right figure shows the distribution of absolute prediction error of the two methods. The distribution seems to be exponential, and the median for the WATS model was less than that of the linear regression model. However, it is clear that the difference between two distributions is not very significant and the performances of the two methods are comparable.

Cross Entropy. From the viewpoint of probabilistic modeling, cross entropy between the distribution estimated by the model and that of the training data set is also an interesting evaluation metric. It is equal to the average negative log-likelihood over the test data. Smaller entropy values indicate better explanations of the data set by the probabilistic model and therefore such a model is considered to be better at summarizing the data. The linear regression is regarded as a Gaussian model; i.e., the target variable follows a Gaussian distribution with mean represented by a linear formula and the variance is a constant. The variance estimator is the variance of the residual in the training data set.

In this evaluation, the linear regression model was trained for each segment, with the hourly weather observation value w being the input value and with the actual travel time being the target value, so that the cross entropy of the actual travel time data can be evaluated. The test data included 56,186,309 observation values from 31,891 segments. The cross entropy for the linear model was 4.57 while that for the WATS model was 3.35 (73% of the value for the linear model), calculated using natural logarithms. This shows that our method fitted the data better than did the linear regression method.

3.4   Discussion

Our model has confirmed that traffic patterns depend on weather conditions as well as time and location. It shows traffic smoothness through the travel time or travel speed distributions under different weather conditions, which are characterized by values such as temperature and snow depth, and the model shows the chronic or weather-sensitive bottlenecks. Road administrators and experts might use this knowledge to improve roads before disaster occurs, or for planning snow removals after a heavy snowfall. Thanks to the mixing coefficient for each road segment and for each weather state in our model, clustering analysis could also be applied over the segments. If it works, it will help us to understand the characteristics for each road segment and time period by grouping similar segments such as "susceptible to snow."

The prediction performance of the expected value using our WATS model was comparable to that with linear regression. This result suggests that statistics such as expected value can be learned by a simple model and that there is potentially a linear relationship between weather and traffic. However, the WATS model reduced the entropy of data and therefore fitted the data better than the linear regression model, which cannot explain the individual data points. It is presumably caused by the multimodality of the travel time distribution. Typically, there are several modes in ordinary roads. Vehicles that pass through the road link without stopping are said to be in "smooth" mode. Vehicles may also stop at an intersection or a traffic signal, so the mean speed slows down in this case; such vehicles are in "stop" mode. Because of this multimodality, the expected value can take a value with a low probability density. In other words, the actual observed values tend to differ from the expected value, and therefore, it seems not to be reasonable to suppose that an observed value is unusual or anomalous just because it differs from the expected value.

Cross entropy is the average information of a data point. Less entropy indicates less information per data point, so that the data become more predictable. In other words, a low-entropy model can regard most of the data as usual. From the entropy evaluation, the proposed model regards larger amounts of data as more "usual" than does the linear regression. Further work is under way to conduct anomaly detection using the WATS model, whereby traffic incidents or sudden bottlenecks could be found in real time.

Our analysis is empirical but represents a first step in understanding the social–physical space. In this paper, we have used travel time as the feature value for the traffic on a road segment and assumed that it follows a gamma distribution. However, feature selection and probabilistic modeling are still open to discuss. Other features such as traffic flow and density, which might be obtained from data sources other than probe vehicles, would be worth considering. Knowledge information such as traffic signal timing will also be helpful to improve graphical model structure and probability distribution functions for mixture components. The model estimation algorithm also requires further development. Model selection, such as determining K and L, is an important open problem. Bayesian inference may also improve model estimation.

4 Conclusion

We have studied a probabilistic model to describe traffic observation data using both traffic and weather conditions. We proposed the WATS model, which is a latent variable model to relate traffic data to weather data by borrowing the idea of the Pachinko allocation model. We have conducted an empirical winter traffic analysis in the city of Sapporo, Japan, by applying the WATS model to real weather and traffic data. The model showed the relationship of the expected vehicular speed to weather conditions, and showed the potential bottleneck segments according to the weather conditions. The quantitative evaluation showed that the WATS model fits the data better than the linear regression model, which suggests the potential for anomaly detection from vehicular observation data.

Acknowledgment. This work was supported by the CPS-IIP Project in the research promotion program for national-level challenges "Research and development for the realization of next-generation IT platforms" of the Ministry of Education, Culture, Sports, Science and Technology, Japan. Weather observation data were provided by the Japan Meteorological Agency. The authors received some information on winter traffic in Sapporo from specially appointed assistant professor Dr. Hajime Imura at Hokkaido University, Japan.

References

1. Bishop, C.M.: Mixture Models and EM. In: Pattern Recognition and Machine Learning, pp. 423–460. Springer, New York (2006)
2. Cao, P., Miwa, T., Morikawa, T.: Modeling distribution of travel time in signalized road section using truncated distribution. In: Proceedings of 9th International Conference on Traffic and Transportation Studies (ICTTS 2014), vol. 138, pp. 137–147. Elsevier (2014). doi:10.1016/j.sbspro.2014.07.189
3. City of Sapporo: Actual budget for the counterplan against snow. http://www.city.sapporo.jp/kensetsu/yuki/jigyou/budget.html. Accessed 30 Nov 2016
4. Guessous, Y., Aron, M., Bhouri, N., Cohen, S.: Estimating travel time distribution under different traffic conditions. Transp. Res. Procedia **3**(July), 339–348 (2014). doi:10.1016/j.trpro.2014.10.014
5. Hall, F.L., Barrow, D.: Effect of weather on the relationship between flow and occupancy on freeways. Transp. Res. Record **1194**, 55–63 (1988)
6. Japan Meteorological Agency: Observations. http://www.jma.go.jp/jma/en/Activities/observations.html. Accessed 23 Nov 2016
7. Keay, K., Simmonds, I.: The association of rainfall and other weather variables with road traffic volume in Melbourne, Australia. Accid. Anal. Prev. **37**(1), 109–124 (2005). doi:10.1016/j.aap.2004.07.005
8. Kinoshita, A., Takasu, A., Adachi, J.: Real-time traffic incident detection using a probabilistic topic model. Inf. Syst. **54**, 169–188 (2015). doi:10.1016/j.is.2015.07.002
9. Lee, J., Hong, B., Lee, K., Jang, Y.J.: A prediction model of traffic congestion using weather data. In: 2015 IEEE International Conference on Data Science Data Intensive System, pp. 81–88. IEEE (2015). doi:10.1109/DSDIS.2015.96
10. Li, W., McCallum, A.: Pachinko allocation: DAG-structured mixture models of topic correlations. In: Proceedings of the 23rd International Conference on Machine Learning (ICML 2006), pp. 577–584. ACM (2006). doi:10.1145/1143844.1143917
11. Tanimura, R., Hiromori, A., Yamaguchi, H., Higashino, T., Umedu, T.: Prediction of deceleration amount of vehicle speed in snowy urban roads using weather information and traffic data. In: 2015 IEEE 18th International Conference on Intelligent Transportation Systems, pp. 2268–2273. IEEE (2015). doi:10.1109/ITSC.2015.366
12. Turksma, S.: The various uses of floating car data. In: Tenth International Conference on Road Transportation Information and Control, pp. 51–55. IET, London (2000). doi:10.1049/cp:20000103
13. Xu, X., Su, B., Zhao, X., Xu, Z., Sheng, Q.Z.: Effective traffic flow forecasting using taxi and weather data. In: Li, J., Li, X., Wang, S., Li, J., Sheng, Q.Z. (eds.) ADMA 2016. LNCS, vol. 10086, pp. 507–519. Springer, Cham (2016). doi:10.1007/978-3-319-49586-6_35
14. Yang, Q., Wu, G., Boriboonsomsin, K., Barth, M.: Arterial roadway travel time distribution estimation and vehicle movement classification using a modified Gaussian mixture model. In: 16th International IEEE Conference on Intelligent Transportation Systems (ITSC 2013), pp. 681–685. IEEE, The Hague (2013). doi:10.1109/ITSC.2013.6728310

Estimating Road Surface Condition
Using Crowdsourcing

Bin Piao[1]([⊠]), Kenro Aihara[1], Akira Kinoshita[2], Atsuhiro Takasu[1],
and Jun Adachi[1]

[1] National Institute of Informatics, 2-1-2 Hitotsubashi, Chiyoda-ku, Tokyo, Japan
{piaobin,Kenro.Aihara,takasu,adachi}@nii.ac.jp
[2] The University of Tokyo, 7-3-1 Hongo, Bunkyo, Tokyo, Japan
kinoshita@nii.ac.jp

Abstract. Road surface conditions have a significant impact on transport safety and driving comfort, particularly in snowy areas. This paper proposes a new method for estimating road surface conditions by using a motion sensor embedded in a smartphone. The method is based on a mobile sensing framework that can collect sensor data using crowdsourcing. In this study, we have defined new road surface conditions as the estimation target, which takes into account both the substance that covers the road surface, and the shape of the road surface itself. The paper also describes a method of feature selection, comprising two steps: First, an initial feature set is directly calculated using various features published in previous studies, using raw sensor data. Second, three feature selection algorithms are compared: Principal Component Analysis (PCA), Relief-F, and Sequential Forward Floating Search (SFFS), and the most effective of the three chosen. In this study, the SFFS algorithm showed higher accuracy than the others. The road surface condition classification was performed across different speed ranges using the Random Forest Classifier, and results show that the best accuracy, of about 91%, was obtained in the 50 km/h–80 km/h range.

Keywords: Road surface condition · Relief-F · SFFS · Random forest · Acceleration · Smartphone · Crowdsorucing

1 Introduction

Road surface conditions are a cause of traffic accidents, particularly in snowy regions, and Fig. 1 shows the winter traffic accident rates for different road surface conditions in snowy areas of Japan; the figure shows that about 50% of accidents have occurred on frozen road surfaces. In areas of snowfall, the road surface can have many different states, which will change with weather and volume of traffic. The changes are mainly influenced by two factors: (1) The substance that covers the road surface, such as asphalt, water, snow, and ice, which is called the road surface type (RST); and (2) The shape of the road surface, such as its roughness or frequency of potholes, which is called the road surface

© Springer International Publishing AG 2017
D. Kotzinos et al. (Eds.): ISIP 2016, CCIS 760, pp. 66–81, 2017.
DOI: 10.1007/978-3-319-68282-2_5

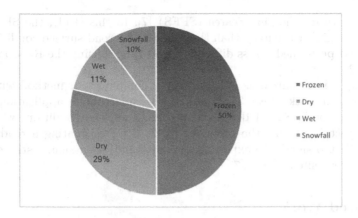

Fig. 1. Traffic accident rates for different road surface conditions

shape (RSS). Most related works on the estimation of road surface conditions focus on only one of these two factors.

Automatically estimating road surface conditions is a critical activity in transport infrastructure management, and many approaches have been proposed. Most make use of expensive sensors to detect road anomalies, or evaluate the road roughness index, however a common problem of these approaches is the high cost of setup and execution. Modern smartphones contain various sensor types such as an accelerometer, gyroscope, and Global Positioning System (GPS), which allow the smartphone to track its position and motion states with a high degree of precision. Because the penetration rate of smartphones is increasing, crowd-sourced mobile sensing, used for collecting low-cost smartphone sensor data, has become possible; this allows for the use of an in-vehicle smartphone to monitor and estimate road surface conditions. Estimating road conditions using such sensors, which are usually loosely placed in the car, nonetheless poses a significant challenge.

Our study proposes a new method for estimating road surface conditions, by using a motion sensor embedded in a smartphone. The method is based on a mobile sensing framework [1], which can collect sensor data reflecting microscopic roadside phenomena using crowdsourcing. In our study, a published smartphone application called "Drive around the corner" is used. This provides an online driving recorder service to collect both sensor data and videos, recorded from the view of the driver; by using this application, users benefit from a free record of their driving, and we obtain large amounts of low-cost sensor data. By utilizing these collected sensor data, the proposed method can estimate road surface conditions which contain both the RSS and RST factors. This paper also describes a method of feature selection, containing two steps: First, to determine an initial feature set we directly calculate various features published in previous studies, using raw sensor data. Second, we compare three feature selection algorithms for effectiveness: Principal Component Analysis (PCA) [8], Relief-F [11,12], and

Sequential Forward Floating Search (SFFS) [7]. In this study, the SFFS algorithm showed higher accuracy than the others. The road surface condition classification was performed across different speed ranges using the Random Forest Classifier [2].

This paper is organized as follows: Sect. 2 compares our method with other related research works; Sect. 3 introduces the smartphone application "Drive around the corner"; Sect. 4 defines a new road surface condition, with some examples; Sect. 5 presents the proposed method for estimating a road surface condition; Sect. 6 shows the experiment results and discussion; lastly, our conclusions are presented in Sect. 7.

2   Related Work

In this section, we give a short overview of other systems used to estimate road surface conditions. These systems can be divided into the following two types: (1.) The use of acceleration sensors to estimate the RSS; and (2.) The use of cameras to estimate the RTS.

2.1   Estimation of Road Surface Conditions Using Acceleration Sensors

For paved roads, most existing work relates to the RSS; for example, the road roughness, or road anomalies such as potholes. The International Roughness Index (IRI) [17] is a standard global index of road roughness, and study [4] shows that the IRI and the Root Mean Square (RMS) of the vertical component of acceleration values, have a high correlation. Using this relationship, it is possible to calculate approximate values of the IRI, however a limitation of the study [4] is that the parameter must be manually adjusted for different vehicles. Another study [19] provides a spring and damper model, which can automatically estimate vehicle parameters including a damping ratio and resonant frequency, and can then use these parameters to calculate approximate values of the IRI. A further study [14] also evaluates the roughness index, but focuses mainly on detecting the changing road conditions. Other research has studied the detection of road surface anomalies, such as potholes; one study [3] provided an improved Gaussian Mixture Model (GMM) for detection of road potholes.

2.2   Estimation of Road Surface Condition Using Cameras

In contrast to normal paved roads, most work on snow covered roads concerns the RST, and uses image processing techniques. Studies [10,15,16] use standard in-vehicle camera devices, such as a driving recorder or smartphone. Among these studies, [10,15] can determine wet or snowy conditions with a high degree of accuracy; however, they cannot detect frozen roads that are the most dangerous in snowy areas. Study [16] can detect frozen roads, but with an accuracy of less than 60%. Study [20] also uses an in-vehicle camera to estimate the road

Table 1. Summary of related works

		Estimation target		Estimation accuracy	Robustness	Estimation cost and granularity
		RST	RSS			
Accelerometer	[3, 4, 14, 19]	×	✓	High	High	High
		×	✓	High	High	Low
In-vehicle camera	[10, 15, 16, 20]	✓	×	Low	Low	Low
		✓	×	High	Middle	High
Fixed camera	[9]	✓	×	High	Middle	High

surface condition with a high level of accuracy, but it is necessary to attach two polarizing films to the lens. Finally, study [9] used a fixed camera placed at representative points on major roads, and to improve accuracy the study also used weather data; the geographical area covered however, was limited.

2.3   Summary of Related Works

Table 1 shows a summary of the related work discussed in this section. A common problem is that no single study supports both RSS and RST. Additionally, approaches using motion sensors such as an accelerometer are more robust than those using cameras. For these reasons, in our study we have estimated new road surface conditions using both the RSS and the RST. Furthermore, we have provided a method to estimate newly defined road surface conditions using motion sensors only.

3   "Drive Around-the-Corner": A Driving Recorder Application

The authors have developed a driving recorder service called "Drive around-the-corner" (Drive ATC); development started in February 2015, and the application became available to the public in February 2016[1]. The function of Drive ATC is to collect behavior logs and event posts, and to deliver information relating to the driver's current position.

The service can be accessed via an iOS application; before driving, users mount their own smartphone, connect a power supply cable if necessary (Fig. 2), and then open the application and start recording (Fig. 3). No further action is necessary, and behavior logs and movies are recorded and uploaded to the service platform while driving.

---

[1] https://itunes.apple.com/app/drive-around-the-corner./id1053216595.

Fig. 2. Smartphone mounting positions.

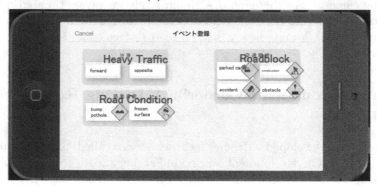

(a) Main Screen

(b) Event options

Fig. 3. The "Drive around-the-corner" application. Traffic information, user-posted events, events extracted from sensor data, and footprints, are shown on the main screen map. (Color figure online)

3.1   User Functions

Map with Event Information. When the Drive ATC application is invoked, it shows a map of the driver's current position (Fig. 3(a)); roadside events are retrieved using the service platform and displayed on the map. For example, the

Table 2. Drive ATC collected data types

Type	Attributes	Sampling rate
Location	Latitude, longitude, and altitude with accuracy	1 Hz
Heading	True_north with accuracy	1 Hz
Move	Speed, course	1 Hz
Acceleration	x, y, z	30 Hz
Rotation rate	x, y, z	30 Hz

yellow icon located at the center of Fig. 3(a) denotes road construction, with the information posted by other Drive ATC users.

Footprint markers indicate previously visited locations, and snow is shown as a triangle. The markers vary with the speed at the position; a shorter triangle denotes slower speed, and a longer triangle faster speed.

Posting Events. To enable users to report a roadside event to others whilst their vehicle is stationary, the application provides a function to post event information. After tapping the footprint marker on the top right corner, users are requested to select an event (Fig. 3(b)). There are eight candidate events in the following three categories: Heavy Traffic, Road Condition, and Roadblock. The selected event is posted to the service platform with the current time and location.

Settings. A menu button to access the application settings is located at the top left corner (Fig. 3(a)). The menu consists of the following list: "about the App", "Movie list", "Settings", "Event list", and "User account". Users can play recorded movies and export them to the general image folder in the movie list.

3.2 Sensing Functions

User Data. The first time a user accesses the Drive ATC service, the following user attributes are collected

- Gender
- Birth year
- Zip code of home town
- Email address
- Nickname

Onboard Location and Motion Sensors. The Drive ATC application retrieves location and motion data from onboard sensors. During driving, behavior logs and movies are recorded, and collected data are pooled in the local data store and then transmitted to the service platform; the types of data collected are shown in Table 2.

4   Road Surface Condition Definition

In this section we explain the definitions used for estimating target road surface conditions. First, we define a set of both road surface types (RST) and road surface shapes (RSS). The set of RST includes four elements: Paved, sherbet, compacted snow, and frozen. The set of RSS also includes four elements: Smooth, bumpy, potholes, and potholes/bumpy. Tables 3 and 4 show details of these; the new road surface conditions are defined by the cartesian product of these two sets.

Figure 4 shows some examples of the defined road surface conditions. Fig. 4(a), (b), and (c) show frozen road surfaces with different RSS. In snowy areas, these are the most dangerous road types; even cars fitted with winter tires may slip. Figure 4(d) shows a sherbet road surface with some potholes; although this kind of road is less hazardous than frozen roads, it will affect vehicle speed. Figure 4(c) shows a road covered with compacted snow; although the road has a covering of snow, driving on this kind of road is usually normal.

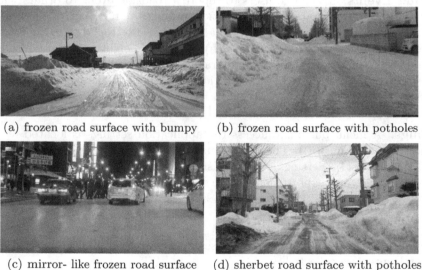

(a) frozen road surface with bumpy   (b) frozen road surface with potholes

(c) mirror- like frozen road surface   (d) sherbet road surface with potholes

(e) flat road surface with snowfall

Fig. 4. Some examples of the defined road surface conditions

Table 3. Road surface type definitions

Road surface	Definitions
Paved road	The road surface is paved with asphalt or concrete, and with no snow or ice on the surface.
Sherbet	The road surface is covered by mixed water and snow ice.
Compacted snow	The road surface is covered with dry snow.
Frozen	The road surface is covered with solid ice or freezing

Table 4. Road surface shape definitions

Road surface	Definitions
Smooth	A flat road surface with no bumps or potholes.
Bumpy	The road surface is flat but has many raised parts.
Potholes	The road surface has some large holes.
Bumpy & Potholes	A mixed road surface with bumps and potholes

5 Proposed Method for Estimating Road Surface Conditions

As mentioned in Sect. 2, most related work has focused only on vertical direction acceleration when estimating road surface conditions, when in fact road surface conditions generate other vehicle in-motion values. Figure 5 shows the raw acceleration data collected for different road conditions. The condition of the left road is frozen and rough, whilst the road on the right is compacted and smooth. When the vehicle is on the left road, acceleration values for both vertical and horizontal direction are greater than for the right road. The reason for the horizontal motion may be due to the car slipping in a horizontal direction despite the driver preference to keep the driving direction forwards only. We can assume from this example that the motion values may reflect both the type and shape of the road surface. If this assumption is true, we can use motion values to classify only road surface conditions that include both type and shape.

In contrast, many studies have used motion values to detect human activities [5,13,18], and changes in vehicle activity may also be seen as a change in road surface conditions; the vehicle activity can then be used to indirectly solve the problem of estimating road surface conditions; the details of the proposed method will be discussed.

5.1 Feature Extraction

In the field of human activity recognition, many effective features have been published using motion sensor data; in our study, these were used as an initial feature set. In our method, signals from each axis of the accelerometer and

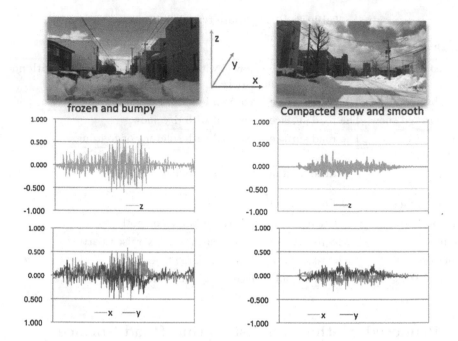

Fig. 5. The number of each road condition at different speed range in the datasets

gyroscope are segmented into windows of 2 s, with a 50% overlap between two consecutive windows. We use x_a, y_a, and z_a to denote the three axes of the accelerometer, and use x_g, y_g, and z_g to denote the three axes of the gyroscope. For both the accelerometer and gyroscope, the x-axis is the direction of the car axle, the y-axis is the direction in which the car is heading, and the z-axis is the vertical direction. Table 5 shows the details of the initial feature set. The extracted features have 67 dimensions in total.

In the field of human activity recognition, the feature "Energy" shown in Table 5 was calculated by using the sum of the squared discrete FFT component magnitudes of the signal. According to [6] human activity often occurs at low frequencies. Therefore, we assume that driving behaviors may also be centralized at a low frequency. In addition, vehicle activity depending on the road surface conditions or the engine vibrations often occur at a high frequency. In this study, to reduce the mutual influence between them, we divided the frequency domain into five equal intervals (from low to high), and calculated the energy associated with each interval.

5.2   Features Selection

A good feature set helps to improve the efficiency of the classification algorithms and enables accurate classification. Numerous feature selection algorithms have been published. Among them, the PCA, Relief-F, and SFFS are three popular

Table 5. Initial set of features for estimating road surface condition

Type of featuer	Features
Mean	$mean_t$ $(t \in \{x_a, y_a, z_a, x_g, y_g, z_g\})$
Standard deviation	std_t $(t \in \{x_a, y_a, z_a, x_g, y_g, z_g\})$
Correlation	$correlation_t$ $(t \in \{x_a\_y_a, y_a\_z_a, z_a\_x_a, x_g\_y_g, y_g\_z_g, z_g\_x_g\})$
Energy	$energy_{t_i}$ $(t \in \{x_a, y_a, z_a, x_g, y_g, z_g\}, i \in [0,4])$
Entropy	$entropy_t$ $(t \in \{x_a, y_a, z_a, x_g, y_g, z_g\})$
Max	max_t $(t \in \{x_a, y_a, z_a, x_g, y_g, z_g\})$
Min	min_t $(t \in \{x_a, y_a, z_a, x_g, y_g, z_g\})$
Mean speed	msp_t $(t \in \{x_a, y_a, z_a, x_g, y_g, z_g\})$

algorithms for feature selection. To select the best features from the initial feature set, we compared these three algorithms to choose the best one. In this study, we determined the criteria of choice as the number of features that provide the best accuracy with the random forest classifiers. For evaluating the accuracy, we used the ten-fold cross-validation approach.

PCA is a mathematical algorithm that reduces the dimensionality of the data while retaining most of the variation in the data set. It accomplishes this reduction by identifying directions, called principal components, along which the variation in the data is maximal. Using this algorithm to select features, we gradually increased the number of PCA components beginning with two PCA components and calculated the accuracy each time for all the 67 PCA components. Finally, the least number of features that provided maximum accuracy were selected.

Relief-F is a filter-based feature selection method used for the weight estimation of a feature. The weight of a feature of a measurement vector is defined in terms of the feature relevance. The features were sorted according to their relevance in decreasing order. The most relevant feature was first added and the accuracy of the given dataset was found using random forest classifiers. Subsequently, the successive relevant features were added sequentially, and the accuracy was calculated each time until all the 67 features were added. Finally, the least number of features that provided maximum accuracy was selected.

SFFS is a wrapper-based feature selection method. It uses a classification scheme as a wrapper around which the whole feature selection is carried out. It starts with an empty set for the desired selected features "X". The features are to be selected from a larger set of features "S". Let's be the most significant feature in S with respect to X, which provides the least accuracy when included in X. At each iteration, the most significant feature in S is included in X if its inclusion does not increase the accuracy. Similarly, the least significant feature in X is found and removed if its exclusion helps improve the accuracy.

5.3   Classification

In this study, we use the random forest classifiers to classify the road surface conditions based on the folders for cross validation. A random forest classifier is an ensemble learning method that constructs a multitude of decision trees at training time. It is one of the most successful ensemble learning techniques that has proved to be very popular and powerful in pattern recognition and machine learning for high-dimensional classification and imbalanced problems.

According to the study [3], different speeds of a vehicle will affect the values of the frequency and the amplitude of the motion, even for a vehicle driving on the same road under the same conditions. In this study, we divided the velocity domain into intervals of 10 km/h. The road-surface condition was classified across different speed ranges using the random forest classifier.

6   Experimental Results and Discussion

6.1   Datasets

The road condition labels were manually generated by three people living in an area of snowfall. The actual ground conditions were determined by voting results from these three people. In addition to the road surface conditions, the acceleration and gyro are also affected by the car, driver, smartphone, and the mount. To reduce these factors, we used the same car and driver, with the same smartphone and mount; differences in motions should thus be affected only by road conditions and driving behavior. We used the dataset from one user, and Fig. 6 shows the numbers of each road condition at different speed ranges. Because the drive recorder application was used during daily driving, imbalances inevitably occurred in the collected data.

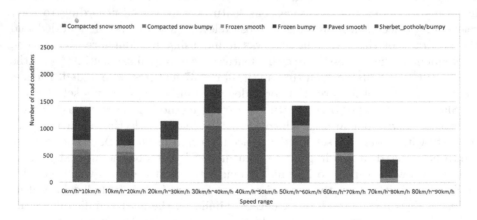

Fig. 6. Numbers of each road condition at different speed ranges

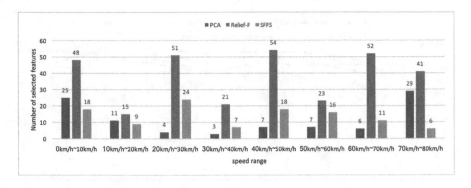

Fig. 7. Selected features from three feature selection algorithms

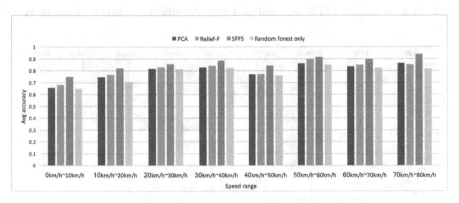

Fig. 8. Performance index comparisons for random forest classifiers, combined with the feature selected algorithms

6.2 Feature Selection and Classification Accuracy

To select the best features from the initial feature set, we compared three kinds of feature selection algorithm: The PCA, the Relief-F, and the SFFS. Each algorithm is evaluated against the accuracy of the random forest, with ten folders for cross validation. The accuracy is defined as

$$Accuracy = \frac{TP + TN}{TP + TN + FP + FN} \tag{1}$$

where TP is the number of true positives, FN the number of false negatives, TN the number of true negatives, and FP the number of false positives. Figure 7 shows the selected features from three feature selection algorithms, and Fig. 8 shows the performance index comparisons for random forest classifiers, combined with the feature selected algorithms; the SFFS algorithm is most effective, with fewer features and higher accuracy in each speed range.

Based on the results above, we decided to use SFFS as the feature selection algorithm. In this study, the classification was evaluated against the recall of the

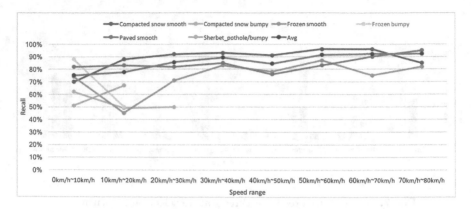

Fig. 9. Results of the SFFS + Random forest classification, across different speed ranges

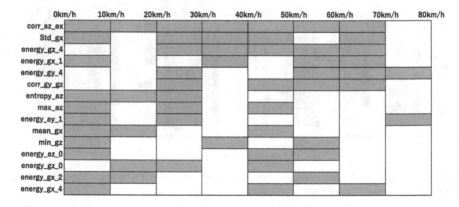

Fig. 10. Details of the selected features by using the SFFS in different speed ranges.

random forest, with ten folders for cross validation. The recall is defined as

$$Recall = \frac{TP}{TP + FN} \tag{2}$$

Figure 9 shows the results of the SFFS+Random forest classification across different speed ranges; The results show that the best average of recall, of about 91%, was obtained in the 50 km/h–80 km/h range. Therefore, we could confirm that the road surface conditions can be effectively classified by using only the motion values when the speed is greater than 50 km/h. In particular, we could confirm that the most dangerous frozen road can be classified by using only the motion values.

Figure 10 shows the details of the major features selected by using the SFFS. The most common features in different speed ranges are the correlation between the directions of the vertical and the car axle, the standard deviation of the pitching of the vehicle, and the high frequency energy.

6.3   Discussion

From the experimental results, we can see that the more complex RSS such as bumpy na potholes are distributed in the low-speed range, and accuracy of the classification between them is very low. One of the reasons is that we have not quantitatively defined the RSS.

In this paper, we have described an estimation method for the road-surface condition by using only one vehicle. However, in the future, we need to estimate the road surface conditions by using multiple vehicles. Many factors influence vertical motion values. One of the factors is the type of vehicle. Length of the wheelbase and the strength of the suspension differ depending on the type of vehicle, and we believe these aspects have an influence on the motion values. The other factor is the individuals driving style. We infer that the motion values change differently, depending on the individuals driving technique and experience. We need to verify the relationship between these factors and the motion values in the future.

7   Conclusions

In this paper, we have proposed a new method for estimating road-surface conditions using motion sensor data. The motion sensor data are collected by a smartphone application called "Drive around the corner." This provides an online driving recorder service to collect both sensor data and videos, recorded from the view of the driver. Using this application, users benefit from a free record of their driving, and we obtain large amounts of low-cost sensor data. The proposed method can use only the collected motion values to classify both the RST and the RSS. In the future, we will consider a method to improve estimation accuracy in full speed range. We will also consider how to eliminate the individual differences between different vehicles or drivers to estimate the road surface conditions by using multiple vehicles.

Acknowledgments. This research was supported by "Research and Development on Fundamental and Utilization Technologies for Social Big Data" of the Commissioned Research of National Institute of Information and Communications Technology (NICT), Japan. And also it was partly supported by the CPS-IIP Project in the research promotion program "Research and Development for the Realization of Next-Generation IT Platforms" of the Ministry of Education, Culture, Sports, Science and Technology of Japan (MEXT).

References

1. Aihara, K., Bin, P., Imura, H., Takasu, A., Tanaka, Y.: On feasibility of crowdsourced mobile sensing for smarter city life. In: Streitz, N., Markopoulos, P. (eds.) DAPI 2016. LNCS, vol. 9749, pp. 395–404. Springer, Cham (2016). doi:10.1007/978-3-319-39862-4_36
2. Breiman, L.: Random for. Mach. Learn. 45(1), 5–32 (2001)

3. Chen, K., Lu, M., Tan, G., Wu, J.: CRSM: crowdsourcing based road surface monitoring. In: 2013 IEEE 10th International Conference on High Performance Computing and Communications & 2013 IEEE International Conference on Embedded and Ubiquitous Computing (HPCC_EUC), pp. 2151–2158. IEEE (2013)

4. Fujino, Y., Kitagawa, K., Furukawa, T., Ishii, H.: Development of Vehicle Intelligent Monitoring System (VIMS), part 1st edn., vol. 5765, pp. 148–157. SPIE (2005). doi:10.1117/12.601727

5. Gupta, P., Dallas, T.: Feature selection and activity recognition system using a single triaxial accelerometer. IEEE Trans. Biomed. Eng. **61**(6), 1780–1786 (2014)

6. He, Z., Jin, L.: Activity recognition from acceleration data based on Discrete Cosine Transform and SVM. In: The 2009 IEEE International Conference on Systems, Man, and Cybernetics, pp. 5041–5044 (2009). http://ieeexplore.ieee.org/xpl/downloadCitations

7. Jain, A., Zongker, D.: Feature selection: evaluation, application, and small sample performance. IEEE Trans. Pattern Anal. Mach. Intel. **19**(2), 153–158 (1997)

8. Jolliffe, I.: Principal Component Analysis. Springer, New York (1986). doi:10.1007/b98835

9. Jonsson, P.: Classification of road conditions: from camera images and weather data. In: 2011 IEEE International Conference on Computational Intelligence for Measurement Systems and Applications (CIMSA), pp. 1–6. IEEE (2011)

10. Kawai, S., Takeuchi, K., Shibata, K., Horita, Y.: A method to distinguish road surface conditions for car-mounted camera images at night-time. In: 012 12th International Conference on ITS Telecommunications (ITST), vol. 2, pp. 668–672. IEEE (2012)

11. Kira, K., Rendell, L.A.: A practical approach to feature selection. In: Proceedings of the ninth international workshop on Machine learning, pp. 249–256 (1992)

12. Kononenko, I.: Estimating attributes: analysis and extensions of RELIEF. In: Bergadano, F., De Raedt, L. (eds.) ECML 1994. LNCS, vol. 784, pp. 171–182. Springer, Heidelberg (1994). doi:10.1007/3-540-57868-4_57

13. Korpela, J., Maekawa, T., Eberle, J., Chakraborty, D., Aberer, K.: Tree-structured classifier for acceleration-based activity and gesture recognition on smartwatches. In: 2016 IEEE International Conference on Pervasive Computing and Communication Workshops (PerCom Workshops), pp. 1–4. IEEE (2016)

14. Nomura, T., Shiraishi, Y.: A method for estimating road surface conditions with a smartphone. Int. J. Inform. Soc. **7**(1), 29–36 (2015)

15. Omer, R., Fu, L.: An automatic image recognition system for winter road surface condition classification. In: 2010 13th International IEEE Conference on Intelligent Transportation Systems (ITSC), pp. 1375–1379. IEEE (2010)

16. Qian, Y., Almazan, E.J., Elder, J.H.: Evaluating features and classifiers for road weather condition analysis. In: 2016 IEEE International Conference on Image Processing (ICIP), pp. 4403–4407. IEEE (2016)

17. Sayers, M.: On the calculation of international roughness index from longitudinal road profile. Transp. Res. Rec. **1501**, 1–12 (1995)

18. Wu, J., Pan, G., Zhang, D., Qi, G., Li, S.: Gesture recognition with a 3-D accelerometer. In: Zhang, D., Portmann, M., Tan, A.-H., Indulska, J. (eds.) UIC 2009. LNCS, vol. 5585, pp. 25–38. Springer, Heidelberg (2009). doi:10.1007/978-3-642-02830-4_4

19. Yagi, K.: A measuring method of road surface longitudinal profile from sprung acceleration, and verification with road profiler. J. Japan Soc. Civ. Eng. Ser. E1 (Pavement Eng.) **69**(3) (2013)
20. Yamada, M., Ueda, K., Horiba, I., Tsugawa, S., Yamamoto, S.: A study of the road surface condition detection technique based on the image information for deployment on a vehicle. IEEE Trans. Electr. Inform. Syst. **124**(3), 753–760 (2004). doi:10.1541/ieejeiss.124.753

Network-Based Pedestrian Tracking System with Densely Placed Wireless Access Points

Ryuta Abe[1], Junpei Shimamura[1], Kento Hayata[1],
Hiroaki Togashi[2(✉)], and Hiroshi Furukawa[2]

[1] Graduate School of Information Science and Electrical Engineering,
Kyushu University, Fukuoka, Japan
{abe,shimamura,hayata}@mobcom.ait.kyushu-u.ac.jp
[2] Faculty of Information Science and Electrical Engineering, Kyushu University, Fukuoka, Japan
{togashi,furuhiro}@mobcom.ait.kyushu-u.ac.jp

Abstract. Demand for care services, especially for children and the elderly, has been increasing. Several GPS-based pedestrian tracking systems have been researched and developed, but GPS cannot provide accurate position estimates in high-rise areas and indoor environments. In order to settle this issue, we propose a pedestrian tracking system that uses Wi-Fi beacons held by target persons and Wi-Fi access points placed widely and densely in a specified area. Target users' positions are estimated on the basis of probe request signals broadcast by the Wi-Fi beacons. The positioning algorithm is based on proximity detection based on received signal strength. In addition, the proposed method uses a computation time reduction strategy and error reduction techniques. Each target's trajectory is estimated on the basis of position estimates using several trajectory correction algorithms. Experimental results show that the proposed positioning system can estimate a target's trajectory with approximately 80% accuracy, with a positioning delay, i.e., time taken to estimate a target's position, of approximately 2.8 s.

Keywords: Indoor positioning · Target tracking · Care service · Wi-Fi · Probe request signal

1 Introduction

Anxiety regarding public safety for children, women, and the elderly is increasing [1, 2]. For example, most Japanese children carry an "anti-crime buzzer" to and from school. The increasing number of aged wanderers has become urgent social issue owing to the rapid aging of the population [3]. Reflecting these backdrops, demand for care services, especially for children and the elderly has been increasing. In outdoor environment, GPS based caring systems are already in practical use [4, 5]. However, GPS cannot provide accurate position estimates in high-rise areas and indoor environment.

The importance of traffic offloading from cellular networks to Wi-Fi networks is also increasing, owing to the rapid growth of network traffic [6] caused by widely distributed smartphones and tablet devices. To expand Wi-Fi coverage areas, large numbers of Wi-Fi access points (APs) are being installed in urban areas, including

© Springer International Publishing AG 2017
D. Kotzinos et al. (Eds.): ISIP 2016, CCIS 760, pp. 82–96, 2017.
DOI: 10.1007/978-3-319-68282-2_6

shopping malls and underground malls. We consider that this AP infrastructure can be utilized for pedestrian tracking systems, to achieve pedestrian tracking system applicable in the environments that GPS cannot provide accurate positioning estimates. This paper proposes a pedestrian tracking system that utilizes widely and densely placed APs. The algorithm is consider to be applicable in indoor environment and achieve high tracking resolution and accuracy.

The remainder of this paper is organized as follows. Section 2 describes research background including brief introduction of related researches. Section 3 describes the proposed system, and Sect. 4 shows experimental results of the proposed system in indoor environment. Section 5 concludes this paper.

2   Research Background

2.1   Overview of Basic Positioning Methods

This section reviews some basic positioning methods. Positioning algorithms are roughly categorized as range-based and range-free. Among range-free methods, the simplest is a proximity-based method that estimates a device's position as an AP's position, on the basis of a proximity metric, e.g., the received signal strength indication (RSSI). The centroid [7] and weighted centroid [8] methods estimate a device's position as the weighted center of the APs whose signals were captured by the device, or else as the APs that captured the signal broadcast by the device. For range-based methods, trilateration uses three known positions and the distances to an unknown position, i.e., the position to be estimated. To estimate distances, RSSI, time of arrival, and time difference of arrival are used. Triangulation uses two known positions and two angles toward the unknown position. This method works with an angle measurement method, e.g., angle of arrival observed using an antenna array.

Positioning accuracy can be improved by taking into account the possible walking paths in a given positioning area for position estimation. Typical examples of positioning methods utilizing this kind of information are as follows. Madigan et al. use a Bayesian graphical model [9] in indoor positioning. Their approach has achieved approximately 5–6 m positioning accuracy while excluding the requirement for training data. C.S. Jensen et al. have proposed a graph model-based approach [10]. Their method uses RFID readers attached to each door in the positioning area and estimates each RFID tag's position using several graphs defined on the basis of the area's floor plan. The results of their simulation suggest that their method can accurately track each RFID tag held by the target pedestrians.

Positioning frameworks can be roughly categorized into device- (terminal) and network-side systems. In a device-side system, a device estimates its own position. An advantage of this framework is that device movement can be directly and precisely observed using sensors on the device. In contrast, the computational and power resources of a mobile device are limited compared to that of standard desktop computers. A network-side system estimates the device position using networked sensors, such as passive infrared sensors or Wi-Fi APs. Each device obtains its position estimates by accessing the network. For example, a device's position can be estimated by observing the signals broadcast by the device on Wi-Fi APs placed in the given area. Advantages of this framework are that software does not need to be installed on mobile devices, and high-performance computing equipment can be used for position estimation.

2.2 Wi-Fi Based Pedestrian Tracking Systems

There exists several pedestrian tracking systems utilizing Wi-Fi signal. Musa and Eriksson's method [11] employs a simple hidden Markov model to estimate device position accurately. However, this method was only evaluated on a granularity of around 100 m, and its evaluation was focused mostly on 1-D placement of APs. Mirowski et al.'s method [12] employs kernel based algorithm in position estimation with using large number of fingerprints gathered in a certain positioning area. Marthisen et al.'s method [13] utilizes radio map prepared on the basis of the previously measured data, to estimate position of pedestrian.

We propose a method to achieve fine-grained pedestrian tracking, i.e., pedestrian tracking inside a building, by utilizing densely placed Wi-Fi APs and eliminating reference data preparation.

2.3 Wireless Backhaul Technology

Small cells are the key technology in setting up a wide Wi-Fi coverage area and achieving large network capacity. To connect small cells to the core network (e.g., Internet), backhaul is essential. However, wired backhaul is inefficient, because all access points are wired to the core network; to achieve wide Wi-Fi coverage areas, huge amounts of cables must be installed.

Wireless backhaul is a wireless multi-hop network in which access points are linked wirelessly with the capability of relaying packets. In a wireless backhaul network, a few access points (we refer to them as "core nodes") are wired to the core network and serve as gateways connecting the wireless multi-hop network to the Internet. Therefore,

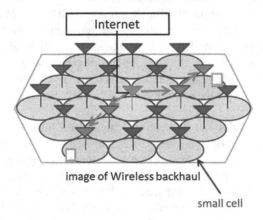

Fig. 1. Simple image of Wireless backhaul network. Wireless backhaul technology enables the setting up of a large Wi-Fi coverage area without laying huge amounts of access cables.

wireless backhaul is advantageous in achieving a wide Wi-Fi coverage area, because this technology can reduce wiring cost significantly. For example, as in Fig. 1, a Wi-Fi coverage area can be set up by placing wireless APs, with only one AP wired to the core network. However, mobile devices in this area can access the Internet, regardless of the AP to which a device is associated.

2.4 PCWL-0200

PCWL-0200 [14] is a wireless local area network (LAN) AP developed in our laboratory that uses wireless backhaul technology. This AP can set up a Wi-Fi coverage area without configuring a relay route among APs manually; the route is determined automatically, on the basis of the radio wave propagation environment, e.g., the RSSI observed between each two APs. PCWL-0200 has been commercialized, and a significant number of Wi-Fi access areas set up by these APs are in practical use.

Another feature of PCWL-0200 is that this AP can capture probe request signals broadcast by surrounding mobile devices. When a core node is wired to the Internet, probe request signals captured around the area can be stored to an online database server via the wireless backhaul network.

2.5 Probe Request Signal

There are two means of establishing connections between Wi-Fi devices and APs, active and passive scanning. In active scanning, a device broadcasts a probe request and listens for a probe response from surrounding APs. A connection can be established, when a probe response is received. Passive scanning uses beacon signals broadcast periodically by APs to establish a connection. Most smartphones broadcast probe request signals at random intervals to run active scanning and establish a network connection quickly. The frequency at which a Wi-Fi device broadcasts a probe request signal differs based on factors such as device type, connection status, operating system, and software. Generally, mobile devices broadcast probe request signals more frequently when it is not associated to an AP, and its display is turned on. The following information can be obtained from a probe request signal:

- Sender media access control (MAC) address
- RSSI
- Extended service set identifier (ESS-ID, only when explicitly declared)

Originally, a MAC address is factory assigned and unique to each network interface. However, recent operating systems are capable of broadcasting probe request signals with randomized address [15]. MAC address randomization by itself does not affect device tracking, but in case that change in MAC address is too frequently, a device becomes difficult to be tracked. Therefore, the proposed system uses Wi-Fi tag that always broadcasts probe request signal with factory assigned MAC address.

3 Proposed System

3.1 Outline

Our pedestrian tracking system uses Wi-Fi APs to set up a positioning area and Wi-Fi beacons that broadcast probe request signals periodically. Therefore, accurate position estimates of each device can be obtained in indoor environment where GPS-based positioning cannot work properly. Each beacon's position, i.e., target user's position, in this area is estimated using a networked server, on the basis of the probe request signals broadcast by the beacons and captured by the APs. The position estimates are stored in a networked database. The trajectories of each beacon are estimated on the basis of the position estimates, with taking the floor plan of the area into account. Consequently, our algorithm can be categorized as a graph-based model; APs correspond to nodes, and routes in the positioning area correspond to edges.

3.2 System Components

The system components are shown in Fig. 2. Each target user holds a Wi-Fi beacon. PCWL-0200 s are used to set up a Wi-Fi coverage area, i.e., a positioning area, and capture probe request signals broadcast by surrounding beacons. These APs transmit these signals to a "positioning server," implemented in Python, via the wireless backhaul network at the request of the server. Note that a single probe request signal can be captured on multiple APs. Each beacon's position is estimated on the positioning server through analysis of these signals.

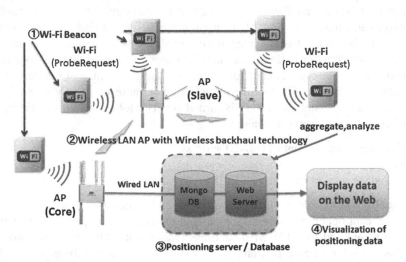

Fig. 2. System components. Each beacon's position is estimated on the positioning server by analyzing the probe request signals captured by wireless APs. Probe request signals are gathered to the server via the wireless backhaul network.

Position estimates are stored in a MongoDB [16] "positioning database." The trajectory of each beacon is estimated from its position estimates and also stored in the database. These trajectories are displayed visually using the D3.js [17] JavaScript library. The web server is implemented using Django [18].

3.3 Positioning Algorithm

The proposed method estimates each beacon's position based on the RSSI values of the probe request signal. Specifically, a beacon is estimated to be located close to the AP that observes the highest RSSI value for the beacon. Position estimates for each beacon are aggregated as a list whose temporal length is within 1 min. This list includes the AP identification number and indicates the route that the beacon has traveled, i.e., trajectory of the beacon.

Positioning accuracy of primitive position estimates is not stable since it is simply estimated based on the measured RSSI values. In order to reduce positioning error, the proposed method uses the following countermeasures:

1. Estimated walking speed
2. Previous position estimates
3. RSSI threshold

Estimated walking speed is calculated from the positioning area route information and the temporal difference between the latest and the previous position estimates. If the speed exceeds a specified threshold (3.9 m/s in the proposed method), the latest estimate is assumed to be an error and is eliminated. This countermeasure reduces errors that occur when the direct distance between two APs is short and no direct walking path exists between them, e.g., opposite side of an atrium or shrubbery. For example, in Fig. 3, a device is sometimes estimated as having traveled from AP19 to AP23, a distance

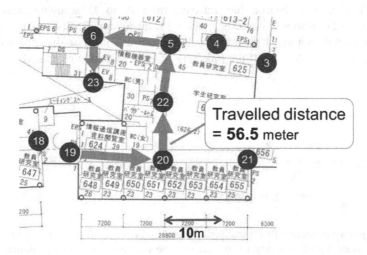

Fig. 3. Error reduction with estimated walking speed. Since a device has been estimated as having traveled from AP19 to AP23 (56.5 m) in 5 s, the latest position estimate (AP23) is eliminated.

of 56.5 m in 5 s. Since the estimated walking speed (11.3 m/s) exceeds the threshold, the latest position estimate (AP23) is eliminated.

Our positioning algorithm is based on RSSI observations. Consequently, a device is sometimes estimated as alternating between two neighboring APs, even though the device actually remains at a fixed position, owing to RSSI fluctuation. The proposed method takes into account the position estimates calculated in the previous 1 min. If shuttling exceeds a specified threshold, then the device is estimated to have stayed close to the AP that observed the strongest RSSI most frequently in 1 min.

A probe request signal can be received by APs located on the same floor as the device and by APs located on different floors. The positioning accuracy can be improved by eliminating the signals observed on different floors. The proposed method also takes into account the RSSI of the probe request signals. Signals whose RSSI values are higher than a specified threshold are used for position estimation. This threshold is set to −80 dBm, which was determined by investigating actual misestimated samples.

3.4   Trajectory Estimation Algorithm

The proposed system estimates each beacon's trajectory on the basis of the spatial series of the position estimates. Primitive trajectory is estimated by simply connecting each position estimate in time-series order. Trajectory estimation accuracy is considered to be improved by taking positioning history into account. Our system uses the trajectory correction by reverse partial match and pedestrian trajectory interpolation algorithms, in order to improve tracking accuracy.

(A) Trajectory Correction by Reverse Partial Match
Each beacon's trajectory is estimated on the basis of position estimates. Therefore, RSSI fluctuation leads to unnatural trajectory estimation, since the proposed system estimates each beacon's position on the basis of the RSSI value of the probe request signals. For example, in Fig. 4, a beacon has traveled from A to D straightforwardly, i.e., A → B → C → D. However, as a result of the RSSI fluctuation, RSSI-based position estimates sometimes do not match the actual walking path, as shown on the left-hand side of Fig. 4, i.e., A → C → B → D. If the trajectory of each beacon is estimated as a simple

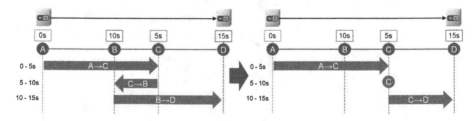

Fig. 4. Trajectory correction by reverse partial match. By considering only the spatial series of positon estimates, a particular target is estimated to be wandering around a particular location, owing to the fluctuation of RSSI. By considering partial trajectory matches, the system reduces unnatural trajectory estimations.

spatial series of the position estimates, the estimated trajectory will sometimes be unnatural. In this example, the beacon is estimated to be wandering between B and C.

To settle this issue, the proposed method considers the reverse partial match between the latest and the previous trajectories in pedestrian trajectory estimation. If the latest trajectory contains reverse partial match of the previous trajectory, this partial match is removed from the latest trajectory; the reverse partial match is considered to be the principal cause of the unnatural trajectory estimation. For example, in Fig. 4, the trajectory between 5 and 10 s partially matches the reverse trajectory between 0 and 5 s, i.e., C → B, and this partial match is eliminated. As a result, the beacon is regarded to be stationary at C in the interval between 5 and 10 s. In the event that a target is actually wandering between specific positions, we can still recognize this situation on the proposed system. In case that a target is actually wandering between A and B as A → B → A → B → A → B → A → B ..., their trajectory is estimated as A → B → B → B → A → A → A → B ...; a person is estimated to be wandering between A and B while staying at A and B.

(B) Pedestrian Trajectory Interpolation

Although a Wi-Fi beacon broadcasts probe request signals every 0.8 s and a PCWL transmits captured signals to the positioning server every 5 s, the system sometimes fails to correct the signal broadcast by beacons, as a result of such factors as radio wave interference or network delay. Therefore, the system sometimes cannot estimate the beacon's position, and its trajectory becomes difficult to estimate. Against this issue, the proposed method uses the following trajectory interpolation method.

In case that the position of a certain device cannot be estimated, the device is regarded to be stayed at a latest position estimate, until the newest positon estimate of the device could be obtained, i.e., probe request signal from the device could be captured again. For example, in Fig. 5, the system cannot estimate a beacon's position at time = 10 s. Because the previous position estimate was B, the system regards the beacon as staying at B. The beacon is regarded as staying there until the next position estimate is obtained. In Fig. 5, the beacon is regarded to have traveled from B to D between time = 10 s and 15 s, because the system could estimate its position at time = 15 s.

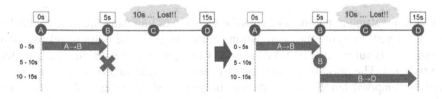

Fig. 5. Example of pedestrian trajectory interpolation. Without interpolation, a beacon cannot be tracked until the signal from the beacon could be observed again. By trajectory interpolation, the system can track the beacon continuously, even if the signal from the beacon could not be observed for a while.

3.5 Data Visualization Framework

Figure 6 shows a screenshot of the proposed system. The main panel (panel 1) displays the estimated trajectory of each Wi-Fi beacon. The filled numbered circles indicate the location of each AP, and the arrows and unfilled circles, colored as shown in the legend, indicate the estimated trajectory of each beacon. The arrows indicate a route each beacon has traveled for a specific duration, and the unfilled circles indicate a location at which the beacon has stayed. In Fig. 6, Beacon 1 (blue) has stayed near AP12, and Beacon 3 (green) has traveled from AP7 to AP5. This panel also has functionalities to show the floor on which each beacon is located, and to change the floor to display estimated trajectories. The floor on which each device is located is displayed in the right hand table of the main panel. This table also indicates the names of users who hold Wi-Fi beacons. Clicking a tab on the main panel chooses the floor of the data to be displayed.

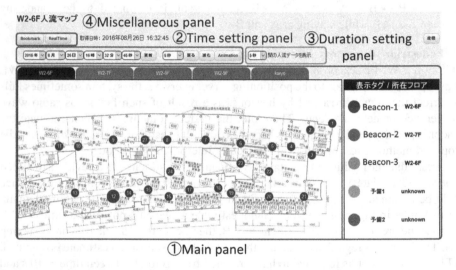

Fig. 6. Screenshot of the proposed system. The arrows and unfilled circles colored as shown in the legend indicate the estimated position of each beacon. (Color figure online)

The time setting panel (panel 2) has the function of choosing the time of the data to be displayed. Pressing the "Animation" button triggers the main panel to update its components automatically; we can visually recognize the routes on which devices have traveled. The duration setting panel (panel 3) has the function of choosing the duration (temporal length) of the data to be displayed. The detailed movement of each beacon can be observed by setting a short duration, e.g., 5 s, and their traveled route can be observed by setting a long duration, e.g., 1 min. The miscellaneous settings panel (panel 4) contains functions to choose among several display settings. The "RealTime" button has a function for switching the main panel to real-time mode, in which the panel shows each beacon's position for the exact current time while automatically refreshing the panel.

4 Evaluation

To evaluate the positioning accuracy of the proposed system, we conduct two experiments, staying and walking experiment. The experimental settings common to both experiments are shown in Table 1. In both experiments, a positioning area is set up using PCWL-0200 APs, and Wi-Fi beacons that broadcast a probe request signal every 0.8 s. Positions of each beacon are estimated on the positioning server every 5 s.

Table 1. Experimental settings. These settings are the same in the walking and staying experiments.

Wi-Fi AP	PCWL-0200
Wireless module of the Wi-Fi beacon	IWM-1101
Broadcast interval of the Wi-Fi beacon (Probe request signal)	0.8 s
Interval of position estimation	5 s

Note that the beacon's position is estimated as the position of a particular AP. Since the granularities of the actual and estimated positions differ, we defined correct position estimates as shown in Fig. 7. This definition is obtained by considering the effect of the RSSI fluctuation of the probe request signals. In the event that the actual position is between APs, both APs are regarded as correct position estimates. For example in Fig. 7(a), AP1 and AP2 are the correct position estimates, when the actual position was at A. In the event that the actual position is within 1 m from a particular AP, this AP and its adjacent APs are regarded as correct position estimates. For example in Fig. 7(a), AP1, AP2, and AP3 are correct position estimates, when the actual position was at B. Further examples of the relationship between the actual and correct position estimates are shown in Fig. 7(b).

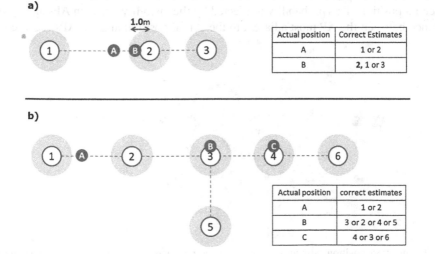

Fig. 7. Definition of the correct position estimates. The position estimates are obtained as the locations of the respective APs.

4.1 Staying Experiment

The physical environment of the staying experiment is shown in Fig. 8. In this experiment, two Wi-Fi beacons were placed at the middles of the straight paths (AP7 and AP20 in Fig. 8) and the intersections (AP5 and AP16 in Fig. 8).

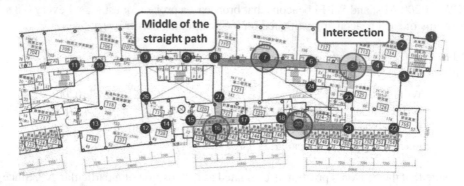

Fig. 8. Physical environment of the staying experiment. The unfilled circles indicate the actual positions of the respective beacons.

The overall accuracy of the staying experiment was approximately 90.5%. Specifically, the accuracy at the middle of the straight path was 90.0%, and the accuracy at the intersection was 91.0%. All incorrect estimates involved the APs the second from the AP most adjacent to the actual position, as shown in Fig. 9. The maximum value of the distance error, i.e., the distance between misestimated results and their most adjacent correct position estimates, was approximately 22.3 m. The occurrence probability of the distance error decreases when the distance error itself increases, shown as Fig. 10. Note that this probability does not include the case in which our system cannot estimate a beacon's position. This probability is affected by the visibility between APs and by the distance between the AP most adjacent to the actual position and the APs regarded as

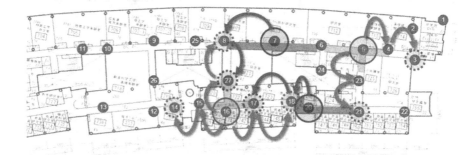

Fig. 9. Incorrect position estimates in the staying experiment. Solid line circles indicate actual positions of Wi-Fi beacons, and dotted line circles show incorrect position estimates. All incorrect estimates involved the APs the second from the AP most adjacent to the actual position.

correct position estimates. We consider that the main cause of these misestimates is the RSSI threshold (countermeasure 3 in Sect. 3.3).

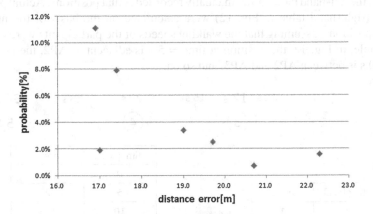

Fig. 10. Distance error of miss estimations. When the distance error increases, its occurrence probability decreases. Note that this probability does not include the case in which the proposed system cannot estimate a beacon's positon.

4.2   Walking Experiment

The physical environment of the walking experiment is shown in Fig. 11. In this experiment, two participants walked along the predefined route three times, holding two Wi-Fi beacons. Their actual walking routes were recorded manually, i.e., each participant recorded the time of arrival at a specific intersection, AP, or other location of interest.

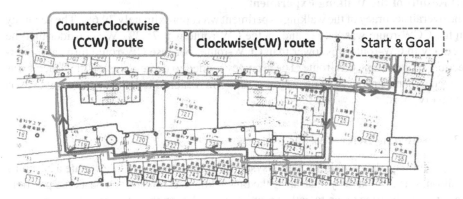

Fig. 11. Physical environment of the walking experiment. Each participant walked along a predefined route indicated by arrows.

(A) Evaluation Method

We compared the estimated and actual positions every 5 s. However, the actual walking route was not always recorded every 5 s, since we recorded the times when participants arrived at specific locations in this experiment. We determined actual positions every 5 s, on the basis of the actual walking routes recorded manually, as shown in Fig. 12. In the figure, the left-hand table shows manually recorded actual positions. Actual positions each 5 s (right-hand table in Fig. 12) were calculated on the basis of the manually recorded positions, assuming that the walking speeds of the participants were constant. For example, in Fig. 12, the position at time = 5 s is adjacent to AP2, the position at time = 10 s is between AP2 and AP3, and so on.

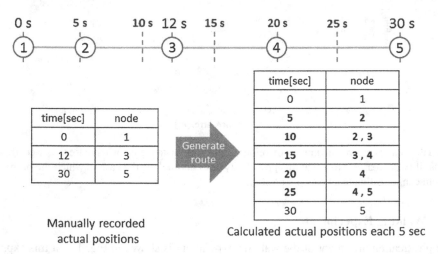

Fig. 12. Determination of actual positions from actual walking routes. Actual walking routes were recorded manually, and the walking speed of each participant is assumed to be constant.

(B) Results of the Walking Experiment

The overall accuracy of the walking experiment was approximately 79.6%. The accuracy on the CCW-route was 84.0%, and on the CW-route was 75.2%. We consider that the accuracy in CW-route was lower than CCW-route, because CW-route turns at a intersection earlier than CCW-route. The accuracy tended to decrease when the beacon was located around an intersection, or on a route on which the distance between APs is relatively short.

4.3   Positioning Delay Analysis

The positioning delay of the proposed system, i.e., the time taken to estimate a beacon's position, was evaluated by measuring the time taken to estimate each beacon's position. Here t_{trans} is the time taken to gather probe request data to the positioning server, t_{calc} is the time taken for the server to estimate the device's position, and $t_{posdelay}$ is the total positioning delay. t_{trans} and t_{calc} are obtained by referring to the log file stored on the positioning server, and $t_{posdelay}$ is calculated as follows:

$$t_{posdelay} = t_{trans} + t_{calc}. \tag{1}$$

The average delay was approximately 2.81 s, and its proportion was

$$t_{trans}:t_{talc} = 3:1. \tag{2}$$

5 Conclusion

This paper shows a pedestrian tracking system using probe request signals broadcast from Wi-Fi beacons. The positioning area was set up using PCWL, a Wi-Fi AP capable of capturing probe request signals and easily extending the Wi-Fi coverage area, owing to its wireless backhaul technology. The system estimates each beacon's position on the basis of proximity detection using RSSI and several error reduction techniques. Each beacon's trajectory is estimated on the basis of the spatial series of position estimates using several trajectory correction algorithms. The experimental results show that the proposed method could estimate a beacon's position with 90.5% accuracy when the beacon is staying at a particular location and could track each beacon's trajectory with 79.6% accuracy.

In the future, we plan to improve positioning accuracy further using the position history of each beacon and to determine more detailed information regarding the given positioning area, including reducing delays, particularly those of the web viewer. In addition, further experiments at practical sites, e.g., shopping malls and underground arcades, will be conducted.

References

1. National Police Agency (Japan). THE WHITE PAPER on POLICE (2016). https://www.npa.go.jp/hakusyo/h28 (in Japanese)
2. National Police Agency (Japan). THE WHITE PAPER on POLICE 2013 – Special Feature II: Police Activities and Children, Women and the Elderly 9. https://www.npa.go.jp/hakusyo/h25/english/WHITE_PAPER_2.pdf
3. United Nations. World Population Ageing 2015 Report. http://www.un.org/en/development/desa/population/publications/pdf/ageing/WPA2015_Report.pdf
4. Location Based Technologies, Inc.: PocketFinder 3G Global GPS + Trackers. http://pocketfinder.com
5. Best 3G GPS Tracker Devices – Trackimo. https://trackimo.com/
6. Ericsson Mobility Report–Mobile World Congress edition, February 2016. http://www.ericsson.com/res/docs/2016/mobility-report/ericsson-mobility-report-feb-2016-interim.pdf
7. Bulusu, N., Heidemann, J., Estrin, D.: GPS-less low cost outdoor localization for very small devices. IEEE Personal Commun. **7**(5), 28–34 (2000)
8. Shen, X., et al.: Connectivity and RSSI based localization scheme for wireless sensor networks. Adv. Intell. Comput. **3645**, 578–587 (2005)
9. Madigan, D., Elnahraw, E., Martin, R.P.: Bayesian indoor positioning systems. In: Proceedings of the IEEE 24th Annual Joint Conference of the IEEE Computer and Communications Societies, pp. 1217–1227 (2005)

10. Jensen, C.S., Liu, H., Yang, B.: Graph model based indoor tracking. In: Proceedings of the Tenth International Conference on Mobile Data Management: Systems, Services and Middleware, pp. 122–131 (2009)
11. Musa, A.B.M., Eriksson, J.: Tracking unmodified smartphones using wi-fi monitors. In: Proceedings of the 10th ACM Conference on Embedded Network Sensor Systems (SenSys 2012), pp. 281–294 (2012)
12. Mirowski, P., et al.: Probability kernel regression for Wi-Fi localization. J. Locat. Based Serv. **6**(2), 81–100 (2012)
13. Mathisen, A., et al.: A comparative analysis of indoor wifi positioning at a large building complex. In: 2016 International Conference on Indoor Positioning and Indoor Navigation (IPIN 2016) (2016)
14. PicoCELA Inc.: PCWL-0200. http://jp.picocela.com/12477.html. (in Japanese)
15. Apple Inc.: iOS Security–iOS 10. https://www.apple.com/business/docs/iOS_Security_Guide.pdf
16. MongoDB Inc.: MongoDB for GIANT Ideas. https://www.mongodb.org/
17. D3.js–Data Driven Documents. https://d3js.org/
18. Django Software Foundation. Django: the web framework for perfectionists with deadlines. https://www.djangoproject.com/

Management of Large Data Graphs

Semantic Partitioning for RDF Datasets

Georgia Troullinou, Haridimos Kondylakis[(✉)],
and Dimitris Plexousakis

Institute of Computer Science, FORTH, N. Plastira 100, Heraklion, Greece
{troulin,kondylak,dp}@ics.forth.gr

Abstract. Today we are witnessing an explosion in the size and the amount of the available RDF datasets. As such, conventional single node RDF management systems give their position to clustered ones. However most of the currently available clustered RDF database systems partition data using hash functions and/or vertical and horizontal partition algorithms with a significant impact on the number of nodes required for query answering, increasing the total cost of query evaluation. In this paper we present a novel semantic partitioning approach, exploiting both the structure and the semantics of an RDF Dataset, for producing vertical partitions that significantly reduce the number of nodes that should be visited for query answering. To construct these partitions, first we select the most important nodes in a dataset as centroids, using the notion of *relevance*. Then we use the notion of *dependence* to assign each remaining node to the appropriate centroid. We evaluate our approach using three real world datasets and demonstrate the nice properties that the constructed partitions possess showing that they significantly reduce the total number of nodes required for query answering while introducing minimal storage overhead.

1 Introduction

The recent explosion of the Data Web and the associated Linked Open Data (LOD) initiative have led to an enormous amount of widely available RDF datasets. For example, data.gov comprises in more than 5 billion triples, the Linked Cancer Genome Atlas currently consists of more than 7 billion triples and is estimated to reach 30 billion [27] whereas the LOD cloud contained already 62 billion triples since January 2014 [25].

To store, manage and query these ever increasing RDF data, many systems were developed by the research community (e.g. Jena, Sesame etc.) and by many commercial vendors (e.g. Oracle and IBM) [10]. Although, these systems have demonstrated great performance on a single node, being able to manage millions, and, in some cases, billions of triples, as the amount of the available data continues to scale, it is no longer feasible to store the entire dataset on a single node. Consequently, under the light of the big data era, the requirement for clustered RDF database systems is becoming increasingly important [6].

In principle the majority of the available clustered RDF database systems, such as SHARD [23], YARS2 [6], and Virtuoso [20] partition triples across multiple nodes

© Springer International Publishing AG 2017
D. Kotzinos et al. (Eds.): ISIP 2016, CCIS 760, pp. 99–115, 2017.
DOI: 10.1007/978-3-319-68282-2_7

using hash functions. However, hash functions require in essence contacting all nodes for query answering and when the size of the intermediate results is large, the inter-node communication cost can be prohibitively high. To face this limitation, other systems try to partition RDF datasets into clusters such that the number of queries that hit partition boundaries is minimized. However most of these systems either treat RDF as simple graphs, exploiting graph partitioning algorithms, [7] or cluster triples based on locality measures with limited semantics [17].

Although RDF datasets can be interpreted as simple graphs, besides their structural information they have also attached rich semantics which could be exploited to improve the partition algorithms and dictate a different approach. As such, in this paper, we focus on effectively partitioning RDF datasets across multiple nodes exploiting all available information, both structural and semantic. More specifically our contributions are the following:

- We present *RDFCluster*, a novel platform that accepts as input an RDF dataset and the number of the available computational nodes and generates the corresponding partitions, exploiting both the semantics of the dataset and the structure of the corresponding graph.
- We view an RDF dataset as two distinct and interconnected graphs, i.e. the schema and the instance graph. Since query formulation is usually based on the schema, we generate vertical partitions based on schema clusters. To do so we select first the most important schema nodes as centroids and assign the rest of the schema nodes to their closest centroid similar to [11]. Then individuals are instantiated under the corresponding schema nodes producing the final partitions of the dataset.
- To identify the most important nodes we reuse the notion of *relevance* based on the established measures of the *relative cardinality* and the *in/out degree centrality* of a node [30]. Then to assign the rest of the schema nodes to a centroid we define the notion of *dependence* assigning each schema node to the cluster with the maximum dependence between that node and the corresponding centroid.
- We describe the aforementioned algorithm and we present the computational complexity for computing the corresponding partitions given a dataset and the available computational nodes.
- Then, we experiment with three datasets, namely CRM_{dig}, LUBM and eTMO, and the corresponding queries and we show the nice properties of the produced partitions with respect to query answering, i.e. the high quality of the constructed partitions and the low storage overhead it introduces.

Our partitioning scheme can be adopted for efficient storage of RDF data reducing communication costs and enabling efficient query answering. Our approach is unique in the way that constructs data partitions, based on schema clusters, constructed combining structural information with semantics. We have to note that in this paper we are not interested in benchmarking clustered RDF systems but only on the corresponding partition algorithm.

The rest of the paper is organized as follows. Section 2 introduces the formal framework of our solution and Sect. 3 describes the metrics used to determine how the cluster should be formulated and the corresponding algorithm. Then, Sect. 4 describes the evaluation conducted and Sect. 5 presents related work. Finally, Sect. 6 concludes the paper and presents directions for future work.

2 Preliminaries and Example

In this paper, we focus on datasets expressed in RDF, as RDF is the de-facto standard for publishing and representing data on the Web. The representation of knowledge in RDF is based on triples of the form (*subject, predicate, object*). RDF datasets have attached semantics through RDFS[1], a vocabulary description language. Here, we will follow an approach similar to [12], which imposes a convenient graph-theoretic view of RDF data that is closer to the way the users perceive their datasets.

Representation of RDF data is based on three disjoint and infinite sets of resources, namely: URIs (U), literals (L) and blank nodes (B). We impose typing on resources, so we consider 3 disjoint sets of resources: classes ($C \subseteq U \cup B$), properties ($P \subseteq U$), and individuals ($I \subseteq U \cup B$). The set C includes all classes, including RDFS classes and XML datatypes (e.g., xsd:string, xsd:integer). The set P includes all properties, except *rdf:type* which connects individuals with the classes they are instantiated under. The set I includes all individuals (but not literals).

In this work, we separate between the schema and instances of an RDF dataset, represented in separate graphs (G_S, G_I respectively). The schema graph contains all classes and the properties they are associated with (via the properties' domain/range specification); note that multiple domains/ranges per property are allowed, by having the property URI be a label on the edge (via a labelling function λ) rather than the edge itself. The instance graph contains all individuals, and the instantiations of schema properties; the labelling function λ applies here as well for the same reasons. Finally, the two graphs are related via the τ_c function, which determines which class(es) each individual is instantiated under. Formally:

Definition 1 (RDF Dataset). An RDF dataset is a tuple $V = \langle G_S, G_I, \lambda, \tau_c \rangle$ such that:

- G_S is a labelled directed graph $G_S = (V_S, E_S)$ such that V_S, E_S are the nodes and edges of G_S, respectively, and $V_S \subseteq C \cup L$.
- G_I is a labelled directed graph $G_I = (V_I, E_I)$ such that V_I, E_I are the nodes and edges of G_I respectively, and $V_I \subseteq I \cup L$.
- A labelling function $\lambda: E_S \cup E_I \mapsto P$ that determines the property URI that each edge corresponds to (properties with multiple domains/ranges may appear in more than one edge).
- A function $\tau_c: I \mapsto 2^C$ associating each individual with the classes that it is instantiated under.

For simplicity, we forego extra requirements related to RDFS inference (subsumption, instantiation) and validity (e.g., that the source and target of property instances should be instantiated under the property's domain/range respectively), because these are not relevant for our results below and would significantly complicate

---

[1] https://www.w3.org/TR/rdf-schema/.

our definitions. In the following, we will write $p(v_1, v_2)$ to denote an edge e in G_S (where $v_1, v_2 \in V_S$) or G_I (where $v_1, v_2 \in V_I$) from node v_1 to node v_2 such that $\lambda(e) = p$. In addition for brevity we will call *schema node* a node $c \in V_S$, *class node* a node $c \in C \cap V_S$ and *instance node* a node $u \in I \cap V_I$. In addition a *path* from $v_1 \in V_S$ to $v_2 \in V_S$, i.e. *path*(v_1, v_2), is the finite sequence of edges, which connect a sequence of nodes, starting from the node v_1 and ending in the node v_2. In this paper we will focus on class and instance nodes due to lack of space, but our approach can be easily generalized to include literals as well.

Now as an example consider the LUBM ontology[2] part shown in Fig. 1 used to describe a university domain. This example contains 20 classes and many properties. Now assume that we would like to partition the corresponding RDF dataset into three partitions revealing discriminating features for each one of them. One way to do that for example would be to identify first the three most importance schema nodes of the dataset, allocate each one of those nodes to the corresponding cluster as a centroid and finally place into the same cluster the schema nodes that *depend* on those selected nodes. The clusters generated using our approach are shown in Fig. 1. The most important schema nodes, as identified by our algorithm, are the *"Professor"*, the *"Publication"* and the *"Person"* classes. These are used as centroids and the remaining schema nodes are assigned to the appropriate clusters by identifying the schema nodes that depend on those centroids. Finally the instance nodes are assigned to the class nodes that are instantiated under. In this paper we will use the term *cluster* to refer only to the schema graph and the term *partition* to refer to the entire dataset.

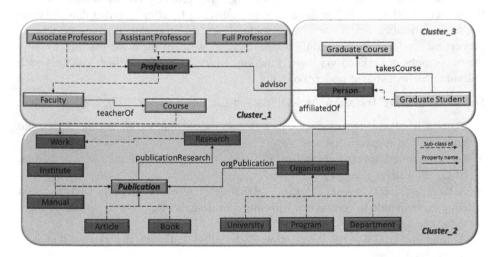

Fig. 1. An example RDF dataset and the corresponding partitions of our algorithm

When data is partitioned across multiple machines the particular partitioning method, can have a significant impact on the amount of data that needs to be shipped

---

[2] http://swat.cse.lehigh.edu/projects/lubm/.

over the network at query time. Ideally we would like the constructed partitions to increase the likelihood that query answers can be computed locally reducing the communication cost. In general, in distributed query processing, where multiple nodes are available, query answering proceeds by first breaking the query into pieces, all of which can be evaluated independently within individual partitions. The query pieces are then evaluated in the relevant partitions obtaining partial matches and they are joined to produce the final answer. Again, in this paper we are not interested on the technicalities of query answering but only on the aforementioned partitioning algorithm and how the careful placement of the nodes within partitions could optimize the overall number of nodes to be visited for query answering.

Assume for example the following SPARQL query involving 3 classes and 2 user-defined properties, requesting all publications of the persons belonging to an organization:

```
SELECT ?X, ?Y, ?Z WHERE{
    ?X rdf:type ub:Person.
    ?Y rdf:type ub:Organization.
    ?P rdf:type ub:Publication.
    ?Y ub:affiliatedOf ?Z .
    ?Y ub:orgPublication ?P .
}
```

If data was partitioned using a simple hash partitioning algorithm, then obviously all nodes would have to be examined. If however, the data was partitioned as shown in Fig. 1 then only two nodes would have to be contacted, as instances of the *"Organization"* and *"Publication"* classes can be found in the second partition and the instances of *"Person"* can be located at the third partition. We therefore, instead of using simple hash or graph partitioning algorithm are looking for a more advanced method, partitioning the schema into appropriate clusters, considering the semantics of the nodes and the structural information of the corresponding graph.

3 Metrics

Our clustering framework follows the K-Medoids clustering method [11]; we select the most centrally located point in a cluster as a centroid, and assign the rest of points to their closest centroids. To identify the most centrally located point in a cluster we use the notion of relevance. Then dependence is used for extracting nodes, highly relevant to the specific important nodes (centroids) connecting other nodes to the most important ones.

3.1 Identifying Centroids

Initially, the notion of centrality [30] is used to quantify how central is a class node in a specific RDF dataset. To identify the centrality of a class node c in a dataset V, we initially consider the instances it contains by calculating *its relative cardinality*. The relative cardinality $RC(p(c, c_i))$ of an edge $p(c, c_i)$, which connects the class nodes c and

c_i in the schema graph, is defined as the number of the specific instance connections between the corresponding two classes divided by the total number of the connections of the instances that these two classes have. Then, we combine the data distribution with the number of the incoming/outgoing edges, aka properties, of this class. As such, the in/out-centrality (C_{in}/C_{out}) is defined as the sum of the weighted relative cardinalities of the incoming/outgoing edges:

Definition 2 (Centrality). Assume a node $c \in C \cap V_S$ in a dataset $V = \langle G_S, G_I, \lambda, \tau_c \rangle$. The *in-centrality* $C_{in}(c)$ (respectively, the *out-centrality* $C_{out}(c)$) of c is defined as the sum of the weighted relative cardinality of the incoming $p(c_i, c) \in E_s$ (respectively, outgoing $p(c, c_i) \in E_S$) edges:

$$C_{out}(c) = \sum_{p(c,c_i) \in E_s} RC(p(c,c_i)) * w_p \quad C_{in}(c) = \sum_{p(c_i,c) \in E_s} RC(p(c_i,c)) * w_p$$

The weights in the above formula have been experimentally defined [30] and vary depending on whether edges that correspond to properties are user-defined or RDF/S, giving higher importance to user-defined ones (in our experiments we used $w_p = 0.8$ for user-defined properties and $w_p = 0.2$ for RDF/S ones). This is partly because user-defined properties correlate classes, each exposing the connectivity of the entire schema, in contrast to hierarchical or other kinds (e.g., *rdfs:label*) of RDF/S properties. Consider now the *"Article"* class shown in Fig. 1. Assume also that there are not any instances in the corresponding dataset. Then the relative cardinality of all nodes is initialized to a constant $a = 0.03$. As such $C_{in}(University) = 0$ since there are no incoming edges and $C_{out}(University) = RC(rdf:type) * w_{rdf:type} = 0.03 * 0.2 = 0.06$.

Now that centrality is defined we are going to define *relevance*. The notion of relevance [30] has been proposed as adequate for quantifying the importance of a class in an RDF dataset. In particular, relevance is based on the idea that the importance of a class should describe how well the class could represent its neighborhood. Intuitively, classes with many connections with other classes in a dataset should have a higher importance than classes with fewer connections. Thus, the relevance of a class is affected by the centrality of the class itself, as well as by the centrality of its neighboring classes. Moreover, since the version might contain huge amounts of data, the actual data instances of the class should also be considered when trying to estimate its importance, namely relevance. Formally, relevance is defined as follows:

Definition 3 (Relevance). Assume a node $c \in C \cap V_S$ in a dataset $V = \langle G_S, G_I, \lambda, \tau_c \rangle$. Assume also that $c_1, \ldots, c_n \in E_S$ are the incoming edges of c ($p(c_i, c) \in E_S$) and $c'_1, \cdots c'_k \in E_S$ are the outgoing edges of $c(p(c, c'_i) \in E_S)$. Then the relevance of c, i.e. $Relevance(c)$, is the following:

$$Relevance(c) = \frac{C_{in}(c) * n + C_{out}(c) * k}{\sum_{j=1}^{k} (C_{out}(c_j)) + \sum_{i=1}^{n} (C_{in}(c_i))}$$

The aforementioned metric identifies class nodes being able to represent an entire area and as a consequence those nodes can be used as the centroids of the corresponding graph. In our example, shown in Fig. 1, *Relevance(University)* = C_{in}(*University*) + C_{out}(*University*)/C_{out}(*Organization*) + 0 = 0 + 0.06/0.048 = 1.25.

3.2 Assigning Nodes to Centroids

Having a method to identify the most important nodes (centroids) in an RDF dataset we are now interested on identifying to which cluster the remaining nodes should be assigned to. Our first idea to this direction comes from the classical information theory; that infrequent words are more informative that frequent ones. The idea is also widely used in the field of instance matching [24]. The basic hypothesis here is that the greater the influence of a property on identifying a corresponding instance the less times it is repeated. According to this idea, we try to initially identify the dependence between two classes based on their data instances.

In our running example, the node "*Person*" has a high relevance in the graph and as a consequence a great probability to be used as a centroid. Assume also two nodes "*SSN*" and "*Work*" directly connected it. Although an instance of "*Person*" can have only one social security number, many persons can be employed by the same employer and as such a person cannot be characterized by his work. As a consequence, the dependence between "*Person*" and "*SSN*" is higher than the dependence between "*Person*" and "*Telephone*". Based on this observation, we define the measurement of *cardinality closeness* of two adjacent schema nodes.

Definition 4 (Cardinality Closeness). Let c_k, c_s be two adjacent schema nodes and u_i, $u_j \in G_I$ such that $\tau_c(u_i) = c_k$ and $\tau_c(u_j) = c_s$. The *cardinality closeness* of $p(c_k, c_s)$, namely the $CC(p(c_k, c_s))$, is the following:

$$CC(p(c_k, c_s)) = \frac{1}{|c|} + \frac{DistinctValues(p(u_i, u_j))}{Instances(p(u_i, u_j))}$$

where $|c|$, $c \in C \cap V_S$ the number of nodes in the schema graph, *DistinctValues*($p(u_i, u_j)$) the number of distinct $p(u_i, u_j)$ and *Instances*($p(u_i, u_j)$) the number of $p(u_i, u_j)$. When there are no instances *Instances*($p(u_i, u_j)$) = 1 and *DistinctValues*($p(u_i, u_j)$) = 0.

The constant $1/|c|$ is added in order to have a minimum value for the CC in case of no available instances. Having defined the *cardinality closeness* of two adjacent schema nodes we proceed further to identify their dependence. As such we identify the dependence between two classes as a combination of their cardinality closeness, the relevance of the classes and the number of edges between these two classes:

Definition 5 (Dependence of two schema nodes). The *dependence* of two schema nodes c_s and c_e, i.e. the *Dependence*(c_s, c_e), is given by the following formula

$$Dependence(c_s, c_e) = \frac{1}{|path(c_s, c_e)|^2} * \left(Relevance(c_s) - \sum_{i=s+1}^{e} \frac{Relevance(c_i)}{CC(p(c_{i-1}, c_i))} \right)$$

Obviously as we move away from a node, the dependence becomes smaller by calculating the differences of relevance across a selected path in the graph. We penalize additionally dependence dividing by the distance of the two nodes. The highest the dependence of a path, the more appropriate is the first node to describe the final node of the path. Also note that the *Dependence(c_s, c_e)* is different than *Dependence(c_e, c_s)*. For example, *Dependence(Publication, Book)* $\geq$ *Dependence(Book, Publication)*. This is happening, since the dependence of a more relevant node toward a less relevant node is higher than the other way around, although, they share the same cardinality closeness.

3.3   The Clustering Algorithm

Having defined both the relevance for identifying the most important nodes and the dependence of two schema nodes we are now ready to define the semantic partitioning problem:

Definition 6 (Semantic Partitioning Problem). Given an RDF Dataset $V = \langle G_S, G_I,$ $\lambda, \tau_c \rangle$, partition V into k subsets $V_1, V_2, \ldots, V_k$ such that:

1. $V = \bigcup_{i=1}^{k} V_i$
2. Let $top_k = \{c_1, \ldots, c_k\}$ be the k schema nodes with the highest relevance in V. Then $c_1 \in V_1, \ldots, c_k \in V_k$
3. Let d_j be a schema node and $d_j \notin top_k$. Then
   $Dependence(d_j, c_p) = \max_{0 \leq x \leq k} Dependence(d_j, c_x) \rightarrow \exists d_j$ in $V_p, (1 \leq p \leq k)$
4. $\forall u \in G_I$, such that $\tau_c(u) \in G_S$ and $\tau_c(u) \in V_j \rightarrow \exists u$ in V_j

The first requirement says that we should be able to recreate V by taking the union of all V_i $(1 \leq i \leq k)$. The second one that each cluster should be based on one of the nodes with the top k relevance (the top_k set) as a centroid, and the third that each node that does not belong to the top_k should appear at least in the cluster with the maximum dependence between the specific node and the corresponding centroid. Note that a node can appear in multiple clusters. The idea originates from social networks where an individual can simultaneously belong to several communities (family, work etc.), similarly an RDF resource might belong to more than one clusters. As such, in order to include a schema node in the V_p cluster $(1 \leq p \leq k)$ we are looking for the path maximizing the *Dependence*. In the selected path however there might exist nodes not directly assigned to V_p. We include those nodes in the cluster as well since they have also high dependence to the centroid. Finally all instances are replicated under the corresponding schema nodes.

The corresponding algorithm is shown in Fig. 2. The algorithm gets as input an RDF dataset and the number of computational nodes (k) and partitions the dataset into k partitions. Bellow we explain in more detail each of the steps of the algorithm.

The algorithm starts by calculating the relevance of all schema nodes (lines 2–3). More specifically for each node in G_S we calculate the corresponding relevance according to Definition 3. Having calculated the relevance of each node we would like to get the k most important ones to be used as centroids in our clusters. Those are selected (line 4) and then assigned to the corresponding cluster (lines 5–6).

Then the algorithm examines the remaining schema nodes to determine to which cluster they should be placed at. For each node we calculate the dependence between the selected node and all centroids (line 7). We select to place the node in the cluster with the maximum dependence between the aforementioned node and the k centroids (line 8). However we are not only interested in placing the selected node to the identified cluster but we place the whole path and specifically the nodes contained in the path, which connects the selected node with the appropriate centroid (*path_with_max_depedence*), maximizing the dependence of the selected node in that cluster (line 9) as well. Next, we add to each cluster the corresponding instance nodes to the schema nodes they are instantiated under. Finally, we return the partitions to the user. The correctness of the algorithm is immediately proved by construction.

To identify the complexity of the algorithm we should first identify the complexity of its various components. Assume $|V|$ the number of nodes, $|E|$ the number of edges

---

Algorithm 1: *RDFCluster(V, k)*
Input: An RDF dataset $V= \langle G_S, G_I, \lambda, \tau_c \rangle$, k the number of the available nodes.
Output: A set S of k partitions $S=\{V_1,..., V_k\}$.
```
1.
2.    for each node c_i ∈ G_S
3.            r_i := calculate_relevance(V, c_i)
4.    top_k := select_top_nodes(r, k)
5.    for each node c_i ∈ top_k.
6.            V_i=V_i ∪ c_i
7.    for each node c_i ∉ top_k
8.            j= find_cluster(c_i, top_k)
9.            V_j=V_j ∪ path_with_max_dependence(c_i, V)
10.   for each node c_i in V_j
11.           V_j = V_j ∪ Instances(c_i)
12.   Return S={V_1,..., V_k}
```

Fig. 2. The RDFCluster algorithm

---

and $|I|$ the number of instances. For identifying the relative cardinality of the edges we should visit all instances and edges once. Then for calculating the schema node centralities we should visit each node once whereas for calculating the relevance of each node we should visit twice all nodes $O(|I| + |E| + 2|V|)$. Then we have to sort all nodes according to their relevance and select the top k ones $O(|V|\log|V|)$. To calculate the dependence of each node we should visit each node once per selected node $O(k|V|)$, whereas to identify the path maximizing the dependence we use the weighted Dijkstra algorithm with cost $O(|V|^2)$. Finally we should check once all instances for identifying the clusters to be assigned $O(|I|)$. As such the time complexity of the algorithm is polynomial $O(|I| + |E| + 2|V|) + O(|V|\log|V|) + O(k|V|) + O(|V|^2) \leq O(|V|^2)$.

4 Evaluation

To evaluate our approach and the corresponding algorithm we used three RDF datasets:

CRM_{dig}[3]. CRM_{dig} is an ontology to encode metadata about the steps and methods of production ("provenance") of digitization products and synthetic digital representations created by various technologies. The ontology contains 126 classes and 435 properties. For our experiments we used 900 real instances from the 3D-SYSTEK[4] project. In addition we used 9 template queries published in [28] with an average size of 6 triple patterns.

LUBM. The Lehigh University Benchmark (LUBM) is a widely used benchmark for evaluating semantic web repositories. It contains 43 classes, and 32 properties modeling information about universities and is accompanied by a synthetic data generator. For our tests we used the default 1555 instances coming from a real dataset. The benchmark provides 14 test queries that we used in our experiments with an average size of 4 triple patterns.

eTMO. This ontology has been defined in the context of MyHealthAvatar[5] EU project [16] and is used to model various information within the e-health domain. It is consisted of 335 classes and 67 properties and it is published with 7848 real instances coming from the MyHealthAvatar EU project. For querying we used 8 template queries specified within the project for retrieving relevant information, with an average size of 17 triple patterns per query.

Each dataset was split into 2, 5 and 10 partitions and we used all queries available for query answering. For a fixed dataset, increasing the number of partitions is likely to increase the number of nodes required for answering queries as the data becomes more fragmented. However, it increases the number of queries that can be answered independently in parallel reducing the computation task for a single node. As we have already mentioned, our task is not to measure end-to-end query answering times involving multiple systems but to evaluate the quality of the constructed partitions with respect to the query answering

As such, for each $V1, \ldots, Vk$ ($k = 2, 5, 10$) we measure the following characteristics: (i) The quality of constructed partitioning algorithms, i.e. the percentage of the test queries that can be answered only by a single partition, (ii) the number of partitions that are needed in order to answer each query and (iii) the space overhead that our algorithm introduces in both schema nodes and the dataset.

We compare our approach with (a) subject-based hash partitioning similar to YARS2 [6] and Trinity.RDF [34] called *Hashing*, and (b) METIS used by [7, 17] for clustering RDF Datasets. *Hashing* is distributing triples in partitions by applying a hash function to the subject of the triple in order to guarantee that star queries can be evaluated locally. METIS [13] on the other hand calculates n disjoint sets of nodes such that all sets are of similar sizes and the number of edges in connecting nodes in distinct sets is minimized. In this work we focus only on the partitioning schemes of the

---

[3] http://www.ics.forth.gr/isl/index_main.php?l=e&c=656.

[4] http://www.ics.forth.gr/isl/3D-SYSTEK/.

[5] http://www.myhealthavatar.eu/.

aforementioned works. All datasets and queries used in our experiments along with the detailed results can be found online[6].

4.1 Quality

We perceive the quality of a partitioning algorithm with respect to query answering as the percentage of queries that can be answered by a single computational node without requiring to visit additional nodes to provide answers to the user. The results for all queries in our three datasets for the three algorithms in 2, 5 and 10 partitions are shown in Table 1.

We can easily identify that RDFCluster is better in almost all the cases showing the high quality of the produced partitions with respect to query answering. The only case that METIS is better than RDFCluster is in LUBM when we have 5 partitions where one more query can be answered by a single one. However, for LUBM, even in 5 partitions as we shall see in the sequel (Sect. 4.2) our algorithm requires less nodes to be visited on average for answering the benchmark queries. In addition we expect that as the number of partitions increases the average number of queries that can be answered by an individual partition decreases as the data are distributed to more nodes. Our expectations are confirmed by our results.

In addition as expected, smaller queries (LUBM with an average of 4 triple patterns per query and CRM_{dig} with an average of 6 triple patterns per query) show a greater likelihood to be answered by a single node than queries with more triple patterns such as eTMO with an average of 17 triple patterns per query.

Table 1. The quality of the three clustering algorithms Hashing (H), Metis (M) and RDFCluster (RC) in 2, 5 and 10 partitions.

Partitions	CRM_{dig}			LUBM			eTMO		
	H	M	RC	H	M	RC	H	M	RC
2	22%	22%	100%	14%	14%	36%	0%	0%	88%
5	0%	0%	44%	14%	21%	14%	0%	0%	13%
10	0%	0%	22%	7%	7%	14%	0%	0%	13%

4.2 Number of Clusters Required for Answering a Query

Besides evaluating the quality of our algorithm, another interesting dimension is to evaluate how much work is required for answering the queries in each case in terms of the nodes required to be visited. The nodes to be visited give us an intuition about how many joins will be required to construct the final answer that will be returned to the user. This is critical because, in order to ensure the completeness of query answers, all partial matches in all partition elements must be computed and joined together.

---

[6] http://www.ics.forth.gr/~kondylak/ISWC2016_Evaluation.zip.

The results are shown in Fig. 3 where we can see that in all cases RDFCluster requires on average less nodes to be visited for query answering, showing again the nice properties of our algorithm. Note that even for large queries (eTMO with an average of 17 triple patterns) our algorithm requires only three partitions to be visited on average for query answering and this applies even in the case of 10 partitions.

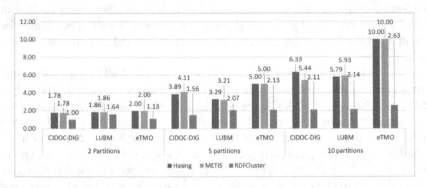

Fig. 3. The number of nodes required for answering the benchmark queries.

4.3 Storage Overhead

The storage overhead provides us with an indication of how much space is needed for our approach compared to the space required for storing all datasets in a single node. Since Hashing and METIS algorithms construct non-overlapping clusters they have no storage overhead. However for simple variations of hash allowing duplication the overhead can be really high (e.g. 2-hop duplication can lead to an overhead up to 430% [7]). In our case, since we allow a class node and the corresponding instances to be replicated in multiple nodes we expect as the number of clusters increases to increase the storage overhead as well.

Table 2. Schema nodes overhead as the number of clusters increases

Clusters	CRM_{dig}	LUBM	eTMO
2	1.55%	3.33%	0.65%
5	1.55%	8.33%	4.90%
10	6.20%	15.00%	7.19%

Table 3. Total storage overhead as the number of clusters increases

Clusters	CRM_{dig}	LUBM	eTMO
2	0.10%	0.12%	0.04%
5	0.10%	0.89%	0.29%
10	16.73%	1.13%	2.78%

To identify and understand the overhead introduced by our algorithm first we focus only on the schema graph and identify the overhead introduced there. This is shown in Table 2 calculating the percentage $|G_{SV1}| + \ldots + |G_{SVK}| - |G_S|/|G_S|$. As shown the overhead is minimal introducing at most 15.00% additional schema nodes for LUBM whereas for eTMO and CRM$_{\text{dig}}$ is only 7.19% and 6.20% respectively.

The impact of these additional schema nodes to the overhead of the entire dataset is shown in Table 3. The table shows the total storage overhead introduced by our algorithm, i.e. the percentage $|V1| + \ldots + |Vk| - |V|/|V|$. As shown, the total storage overhead introduced from our algorithm is at most 16.73% for CRMdig and for the majority of the cases less than 1%. Another interesting observation is that in almost all the cases the schema nodes overhead is greater than the corresponding total storage overhead showing that our algorithm succeeds in replicating only nodes with small additional overhead that however significantly improve query answering as shown in previous sections.

Overall, as the experiments show although our algorithm chooses to sacrifice equal data distribution on the nodes to achieve a better performance with respect to query answering the imposed overhead is really low reaching at most 16.73% overhead on our test cases.

5 Related Work

Graph clustering has received much attention over the latest years [35], aiming to partition large graphs into several densely connected components, with many application such as community detection in social networks, identification of interactions in protein interaction networks etc. The problem proved to be an NP-complete problem [5]. Typical algorithms of this class include local search based solutions (such as KL [15] and FM [4]), which swap heuristically selected pairs of nodes, simulated annealing [8], and genetic algorithms [3]. Algorithms in this category focus on the topological structure of a graph so that each partition achieves a cohesive internal structure and there are approaches based on normalized-cut [26], modularity [20], structural density [33], attribute similarity [29] or combinations between those [35]. To scale up to graphs with millions of nodes, multi-level partitioning solutions, such as Metis [13], Chaco [9], and Scotch [22], and variations over these have been proposed.

To this direction, several approaches try to represent RDF datasets as graphs and exploit variations of the aforementioned data for data partitioning. For example, Wang et al. [31] focus on providing semantic-aware highly parallelized graph partitioning algorithms for generic-purpose distributed memory systems whereas Huang et al. [7] apply graph partitioning over the Hadoop MapReduce framework trying to reduce as much as possible the communication costs. Our approach however, does not focus only on the structural part of the graph for partitioning the RDF datasets but considers in addition semantic information (such as the number of instances, the distinct instance values, assigns different weights according to the type of the properties) with the same target however, i.e. to reduce as much as possible the communication costs among partitions when these partitions are used for query answering.

Other clustered RDF database systems, such as SHARD [23], YARS2 [6], and Virtuoso [20] partition triples across multiple nodes using hash functions. However, portioning data using hashing requires a lot of communication overhead for query answering since in essence all nodes have to be contacted. The same problem appear in other works that adopt vertical [2] or horizontal partitioning schemes based on triples [18] ignoring however the correlation between triples, leading to a large number of join operators among the compute nodes. Other algorithms, but with the same problem use hybrid hierarchical clustering [19] combining an affinity propagation clustering algorithm and the k-Means clustering algorithms. To overcome that problem Lee et al. [17] proposed to by use locality sensitive hashing schemes. Although this approach moves to the same direction with ours, trying to exploit semantics, the adopted solution is limited to only the fact that triples are anchored at the same subject or object node. In addition according to our experiments our solution outperforms similar approaches.

Finally there are approaches that try to monitor the execution of SPARQL queries [1] or assume that query patterns are already available [32] and keep track of records that are co-accessed and physically cluster them using locality sensitive hashing schemes. Our approach uses a similar "profiling" mechanism but instead of focusing on queries, we focus on profiling "data" identifying and combining the knowledge of the instance distribution with structure and semantics. A more thorough overview of the different partition schemes for RDF datasets can be found on [10].

6 Conclusions and Future Work

In this paper we present a novel method that gets as input and RDF dataset and the number of available computational nodes and returns a set of partitions to be stored on the aforementioned nodes. To select the centroids for the each cluster initially our algorithm selects the most important nodes based on the notion of relevance. Then to assign the remaining nodes to a cluster we use the notion of dependence eventually assigning the remaining schema nodes to the cluster maximizing the dependence with the corresponding centroid. Having constructed the appropriate "schema clusters" we place next the instances on the corresponding classes they belong to. Our algorithm exploits both structural and semantic information in order to both select the most important nodes and then to assign the remaining nodes to the proper clusters. In addition, since both our constructed clusters and user queries are based on schema information we argue that this partitioning scheme will have a beneficial impact on query evaluation limiting significantly the nodes that should be visited to answer frequent queries.

The quality of our partitioning scheme is verified by our experiments. We use three RDF Datasets, namely CRM_{dig}, LUBM and eTMO with their corresponding template queries and we show that the clusters produced significantly limit the number of clusters to be contacted for query answering. Obviously, as the number of clusters increases, eventually the number of nodes required for query answering increases as well, leading to trade-offs among load-balancing and the number of nodes to be used. However, as shown, our algorithm achieves better performance than existing systems with respect to query answering, requiring at most 3 nodes for our template queries even when the dataset is partitioned in 10 nodes. In addition, although in order to these results we allow replication, we show that the impact is minimal imposing at most at most 16.73% total storage overhead.

As future work we intend to explore how our algorithm shall be adapted when no schema is available in an RDF dataset; it is true that RDF datasets do not have always a predefined schema which limits their use to express queries or to understand their content. To this direction approaches are starting to emerge discovering the types of the data using clustering algorithms [14]. Furthermore, we plan to deploy our clustering algorithm in a real clustered environment and to measure the actual improvement on query execution times, comparing our solution with other competitive approaches. In addition our clustering method does not considers limiting the number of nodes that are included in each cluster. However, an idea would be to try to limit the nodes assigned to each cluster trying in parallel to maximize the total dependence of the selected nodes. The problem is well-known to be NP-complete, requires complex variation algorithms over Steiner-Tree problem and we have already started to explore interesting approximations [21]. Obviously as the size and complexity of data increases, partitioning schemes are becoming more and more important and several challenges remain to be investigated in the near future.

Acknowledgements. This research is implemented through IKY scholarships programme and co-financed by the European Union and Greek national funds through the action entitled "Reinforcement of Postdoctoral Researchers", in the framework of the Operational Programme "Human Resources Development Program, Education and Lifelong Learning" of the National Strategic Reference Framework (NSRF) 2014–2020.

References

1. Aluç, G., Özsu, M.T., Daudjee, K.: Clustering RDF databases using tunable-LSH. CoRR abs/1504.02523 (2015)
2. Álvarez-García, S., Brisaboa, N.R., Fernández, J.D., Martínez-Prieto, M.A., Navarro, G.: Compressed vertical partitioning for efficient RDF management. Knowl. Inf. Syst. **44**(2), 439–474 (2015)
3. Bui, T.N., Moon, B.R.: Genetic algorithm and graph partitioning. IEEE Trans. Comput. **45**(7), 841–855 (1996)
4. Fiduccia, C.M., et al.: A linear-time heuristic for improving network partitions. In: DAC (1982)
5. Garey, M.R., Johnson, D.S., Stockmeyer, L.J.: Some simplified NP-complete problems. In: STOC (1974)
6. Harth, A., Umbrich, J., Hogan, A., Decker, S.: YARS2: a federated repository for querying graph structured data from the web. In: Aberer, K., et al. (eds.) ASWC/ISWC -2007. LNCS, vol. 4825, pp. 211–224. Springer, Heidelberg (2007). doi:10.1007/978-3-540-76298-0_16
7. Huang, J., Abadi, D.J., Ren, K.: Scalable SPARQL querying of large RDF graphs. PVLDB **4**(11), 1123–1134 (2011)
8. Johnson, D.S., Aragon, C.R., McGeoch, L.A., et al.: Optimization by simulated annealing: an experimental evaluation. part i, graph partitioning. Oper. Res. **37**, 865–892 (1989)
9. Hendrickson, B., Leland, R.: The chaco user's guid, version 2.0. Technical report SAND94–2692, Sandia National Laboratories (1995)

10. Kaoudi, Z., Manolescu, I.: RDF in the clouds: a survey. VLDB J. **24**(1), 67–91 (2015)
11. Kaufman, L., Rousseeuw, P.J.: Clustering by means of medoids. Statistical Data Analysis based on the L1 Norm (1987)
12. Karvounarakis, G., Alexaki, S., Christophides, V., Plexousakis, D., Scholl, M.: RQL: a declarative query language for RDF. In: WWW (2002)
13. Karypis, G., Kumar, V.: A fast and high quality multilevel scheme for partitioning irregular graphs. SIAM J. Sci. Comput. **20**(1), 359 (1999)
14. Kellou-Menouer, K., Kedad, Z.: A clustering based approach for type discovery in RDF data sources. In: EGC (2015)
15. Kernighan, B., Lin, S.: An efficient heuristic procedure for partitioning graphs. Bell Syst. J. **49**, 291–307 (2013)
16. Kondylakis, H., Spanakis, M., Sfakianakis, S., et al.: Digital patient: personalized and translational data management through the MyHealthAvatar EU project. In: EMBC (2015)
17. Lee, K., Liu, L.: Scaling queries over big RDF graphs with semantic hash partitioning. PVLDB **6**(14), 1894–1905 (2013)
18. Lee, K., Liu, L., Tang, Y., Zhang, Q., Zhou, Y.: Efficient and customizable data partitioning framework for distributed big RDF data processing in the cloud. In: CLOUD (2013)
19. Leng, Y., Chen, Z., Zhong, F., Zhong, H.: BRDPHHC: A Balance RDF data partitioning algorithm based on hybrid hierarchical clustering. In: HPCC/CSS/ICESS (2015)
20. Newman, M.E.J., Girvan, M.: Finding and evaluating community structure in networks. Phys. Rev. E **69**, 026113 (2004)
21. Pappas, A., Troullinou, G., Roussakis, G., Kondylakis, H., Plexousakis, D.: Exploring importance measures for summarizing RDF/S KBs. In: Blomqvist, E., Maynard, D., Gangemi, A., Hoekstra, R., Hitzler, P., Hartig, O. (eds.) ESWC 2017. LNCS, vol. 10249, pp. 387–403. Springer, Cham (2017). doi:10.1007/978-3-319-58068-5_24
22. Pellegrini, F., Roman, J.: Scotch: a software package for static mapping by dual recursive bipartitioning of process and architecture graphs. In: Liddell, H., Colbrook, A., Hertzberger, B., Sloot, P. (eds.) HPCN-Europe 1996. LNCS, vol. 1067, pp. 493–498. Springer, Heidelberg (1996). doi:10.1007/3-540-61142-8_588
23. Rohloff, K., Schantz, R.E.: High-performance, massively scalable distributed systems using the MapReduce software framework: the SHARD triple-store. In: PSI EtA, 4 (2010)
24. Seddiqui, H., Nath, R.P.D., Aono, M.: An efficient metric of automatic weight generation for properties in instance matching technique. JWS **6**(1), 1–17 (2015)
25. Schmachtenberg, M., Bizer, C., Paulheim, H.: State of the LOD Cloud. http://linkeddatacatalog.dws.informatik.uni-mannheim.de/state/. Accessed 30 Apr 2016
26. Shi, J., Malik, J.: Normalized cuts and image segmentation. IEEE Trans. Pattern Anal. Mach. Intell. **22**(8), 888–905 (2000)
27. The Cancer Genome Atlas project. http://cancergenome.nih.gov/. Accessed 30 Apr 2016
28. Theodoridou, M., Tzitzikas, Y., Doerr, M., et al.: Modeling and querying provenance by extending CIDOC CRM. Distrib. Parallel Databases **27**(2), 169–210 (2010)
29. Tian, Y., Hankins, R.A., Patel, J.M.: Efficient aggregation for graph summarization. In: SIGMOD (2008)
30. Troullinou, G., Kondylakis, H., Daskalaki, E., Plexousakis, D.: RDF digest: efficient summarization of RDF/S KBs. In: Gandon, F., Sabou, M., Sack, H., d'Amato, C., Cudré-Mauroux, P., Zimmermann, A. (eds.) ESWC 2015. LNCS, vol. 9088, pp. 119–134. Springer, Cham (2015). doi:10.1007/978-3-319-18818-8_8
31. Wang, L., Xiao, Y., Shao, B., Wang, H.: How to partition a billion-node graph. In: ICDE (2014)
32. Wang, X., Yang, T., Chen, J., He, L., Du, X.: RDF partitioning for scalable SPARQL query processing. Front. Comput. Sci. **9**(6), 919–933 (2015)

33. Xu, X., Yuruk, N., Feng, Z., Schweiger, T.A.J.: Scan: a structural clustering algorithm for networks. In: KDD (2007)
34. Zeng, K., Yang, J., Wang, H., Shao, B., Wang, Z.: A distributed graph engine for web scale RDF data. PVLDB **6**(4), 265–276 (2013)
35. Zhou, Y., Cheng, H., Yu, J.X.: Graph clustering based on structural/attribute similarities. PVLDB **2**(1), 718–729 (2009)

Personal Networks of Scientific Collaborators: A Large Scale Experimental Analysis of Their Evolution

Sarra Djemili[1,2]($\boxtimes$), Claudia Marinica[1], Maria Malek[2], and Dimitris Kotzinos[1]

[1] ETIS Lab UMR 8051 University of Paris-Seine, University of Cergy-Pontoise, ENSEA, CNRS, Cergy-Pontoise, France
{sarra.djemili,claudia.marinica}@ensea.fr,
dimitrios.kotzinos@u-cergy.fr
[2] QUARTZ Lab - EISTI, Cergy-Pontoise, France
mma@eisti.eu

Abstract. When an individual joins an Online Social Network (OSN), he creates connections by interacting with the other users directly or indirectly and forms its own Online Personal Network (OPN). These OPNs are not static, but they evolve over time as new people join or quit them and as new relationships are established or old ones broken. Understanding how OPNs are evolving is still missing in the current literature, while OSNs' evolution was widely addressed and many models were proposed. In this paper, we propose to fill this gap by performing an experimental analysis over a large set of real OPNs by the mean of the computation of metrics that characterize their structure. We examine how these metrics behave when the OPNs change over time in order to discover the properties driving the evolution of their structure, which can help in providing evolution models dedicated to OPNs.

Keywords: Online personal networks · Online personal networks evolution · Network dynamics · Online social networks · Graph metrics

1 Introduction

An Online Social Network (OSN) consists of a set of nodes that represent the actors (e.g. the persons) involved in the network, while the edges connecting the nodes represent (online) social relationships like friendship, family, work and others. At the same time, each individual belonging to an OSN has its own Online Personal or Egocentric Network composed of that node/user as its focal point (named ego) and of these users that the ego is interacting with directly or indirectly (named alters).

But, OSNs carry many dynamic characteristics and they change over time in terms both of structure (e.g. nodes or connections with other nodes are added/deleted) and weight of the links (e.g. strength of exchanges between two nodes). Understanding the dynamic nature of OSNs has been widely addressed in

D. Kotzinos et al. (Eds.): ISIP 2016, CCIS 760, pp. 116–139, 2017.
DOI: 10.1007/978-3-319-68282-2_8

the literature and many models were proposed to capture this evolution. Most of these models are based on properties that concern the OSN structure as a whole, e.g. the global clustering coefficient. But for us as individuals, what happens to the whole network is less important than what happens to our corner of this online world. So, we are more interested on how our personal network will evolve over time and how this evolution will affect us in terms of our local communities or the information that will reach us. Thus, in contrast with the prevailing approach of studying the evolution of the whole OSNs, we are interested in extracting from the OSN the individuals' OPNs and study the dynamics of each personal network individually to understand the evolution at the individual user level. Our goal is to analyze an adequate number of personal networks that would allow us to draw reproducible conclusions (if any) and at the end quantify these conclusions in the form of an evolutionary model.

The dynamics of personal networks can provide insights at various levels. Firstly, at the level of the ego, we are interested in finding how the ego is affecting or is affected by his alters over time and how this affects the evolution of the entire OSN. For instance, it has been demonstrated that the health of a person is strongly related with the number of friends the person has [19], and the identification of influential individuals inside an online social network can lead marketing strategy's decisions [10]. Secondly, at the level of the personal network, we are interested in finding if and how different sub-circles are been developing as the network evolves and how this affects the importance of the ego in the functioning of the personal network.

However, only few works were dedicated to the study of OPNs dynamics. These works focused mainly on: (1) checking if the discovered patterns that characterized evolving human relationships over time in *offline personal networks* (i.e., personal networks as studied in social sciences to represent relationships of a person in the real society) are valid when we switch to online personal networks; (2) analyzing OPNs in specific online applications (for example Facebook or Twitter individually) to detect and describe the different phases about the activity of a user over time after joining the OSN; or (3) providing software that offer visualization support in order to analyze a given isolated evolving personal network. Nevertheless, we are still missing contributions that allow to know more about the structural properties of OPNs.

In this paper, we describe an experimental analysis over a set of OPNs that evolve over time. They are extracted from a greater coauthors OSN that captures collaboration among scientists who have coauthored at least a journal or conference publication. The analysis consists of computing a set of metrics over the selected OPNs for different time steps that correspond to years in real life. The metrics capture information about the ego, the relationship between the ego and its alters, the overall importance of the ego, but also information on alters' connectedness, their local structure, and the appearance of sub-communities. For each metric, we provide the prevailing behavior as the OPN evolves but also we explain this behavior, where possible, in terms of what we know from the literature on network evolution in general, personal networks and evolution of coauthors' social networks. Our goal is to understand the properties and their trends that characterize or explain the changes that personal networks sustain over time. In a future work, we plan to quantify and mathematically describe the trends of these properties so as to be able to propose an evolution model for OPNs. To the best of our knowledge, this is the first effort that tries to perform large scale analytics on evolving OPNs in an effort to understand and capture the dynamics of such networks.

The remainder of this paper is structured as following: in Sect. 2, we define formally an OPN, and in Sect. 3, we review a set of works that have studied OPNs evolution. In Sect. 4, we describe the set of metrics we used in our analysis, and in Sect. 5, we describe the evolution study that we carried and the evolution trends detected via the analysis per metric. Finally, in Sect. 6 we discuss the discovered properties from the studied evolving OPNs, and we conclude with Sect. 7.

2   Preliminaries

As stated in the introduction, a personal network is a network that has an individual as its focal user (named ego) and the users that are directly or indirectly connected to him (named alters). In our previous work [6], we provided a set of formal definitions for OPNs that account for the different characteristics of today's OSNs. Next, we provide the definition of an OSN and then we report the definition of an undirected personal network.

Definition 1. *An (undirected) Online Social Network is a graph $G(V, E)$ where V is the set of nodes representing the social actors and E is the set of (undirected) edges representing the links between them.*

Definition 2. *We define an undirected personal network PN^e of an ego (aka individual node) e as being a sub-network of an online social network composed of the ego and the individuals who are connected to it directly or indirectly (named alters), and of all the connections between e and his alters, and between the alters.*

$$PN^e = G'(V', E'), where V' \subseteq V, E' \subseteq E$$
$$V' = \{x \in V \mid d_G(e, x) \leq k \ \wedge \exists y \in V, \ d_G(e, y) = k\} \cup \{e\}$$
$$E' = \{\{x, y\} \in E \mid x \in V' \wedge y \in V'\}$$

where V' represents the set of nodes composed of the ego node e and all nodes that are connected to e via a shortest path of maximum length k , with the condition that at least one node y is at a k distance from e, and E' holds the set of all possible edges linking V''s nodes. The shorted path is computed by $d_G(e, x)$ as the number of edges contained in the shortest path connecting e to x.

In Fig. 2-a, we give an example of a personal network where the ego is the node in the center of the graph and the set of alters is composed of nodes 2, 3, 4, 5, 6, and 7. Each node is at a distance one from the ego, so, for this personal network, $k = 1$. In contrast, for the personal network in Fig. 2-b, since $d_G(ego, 8) = 2$, $k = 2$.

In this paper, we use Definition 2 for the extraction of personal networks from the entire undirected social network of scientific collaborations, in order to observe and analyse the evolution of a set of individual authors' personal networks.

3 Literature Review

In the last years, numerous studies in OSN analysis has been devoted to understand their evolution over time. These works tempted to develop generative models for large networks that reproduce the properties revealed by the analysis of different online networks, such as their scale-free nature in degree distribution, their high clustering coefficient, and their low average shortest path length that separates nodes (so called the *small-world* phenomenon [22,23]). However, studies on understanding the evolution of OPNs are still young and only a few works were devoted to that.

For example, in [2], the authors aimed to discover how the size and the structure of personal networks' layers change over time. In social science [21], a layer is composed of the alters having the same degree of intimacy with the ego. Using Twitter data in order to assess whether offline personal networks' properties are also valid in Twitter's OPNs, the authors outlined that the number of active relationships maintained by the ego remains constant due to the limited cognitive capacity of human brain. Furthermore, they noted that when the ego joins the OSN, the number of ego's relationships shows an important burst that converges to a constant value. The number of strong relationships is small and is maintained over time, but most of the relationships become weaker shortly after their creation. The later has also been observed in [24] that analyzed the evolution of the Facebook interaction graph and found that different personal networks' links are rapidly activated and deactivated exhibiting a decreasing strength (i.e. decreasing number of exchanges) and that this starts soon after they were created.

Although these conclusions can be helpful when modeling the evolution of relationships' strength in personal networks, they remain limited since they do not reflect how OPNs graph structure is affected over time when nodes and edges are added or deleted. Moreover, by considering only the relationships between the individual (ego) and his direct connections (personal networks with $k = 1$), these studies restrict the information about the evolution of the personal network since many times the evolution appears not on the 1-level but on levels 2 and above.

Visualization techniques help in understanding the evolution of OPNs. In that respect, in [20] the authors propose techniques to visualize large scale personal networks evolution by considering the data as continuous streams, and the visualization software *EgoLines*, presented in [27], proposes a dynamic analysis of personal networks. These tools allow to isolate a personal network and analyze its evolution with a visual support, but they are lacking the capabilities of performing massive scale analysis. The system *EgoSlider* [26] allows the analysis of a set of dynamic personal networks by summarizing their properties at the network, individual or temporal-based level. Unfortunately, the integrated metrics (e.g. number of alters, edges between alters, etc.) are limited and provide only generic information about the OPN.

As in this paper we are interested in understanding the factors that govern the evolution of OPNs by making a large-scale study, we use the expanded definitions of OPNs beyond the immediate social cycle (or for $k \geq 1$), and we focus on understanding: (i) the evolution of ego node's properties and (ii) the evolution of the personal network's structure. We do this by studying a set of metrics that represent key information at both evolution points. In that respect, we follow the analytical work done for the full OSN in [3] where the evolution of scientific collaborations network data was studied by the mean of graph metrics. Compared to this work, we use similar metrics (adapted to personal networks in our case) and we work on similar data sets since both works consider co-authorship networks from the DBLP data set. The metrics that we use for understanding the evolution of OPNs are presented in the next section.

4   Metrics for the Analysis of OPNs Evolution

As outlined previously, we can use metrics that describe the structure of the OPNs to capture its evolution and get insights on how personal networks grow, shrink or change over time. From the many metrics proposed in the literature for capturing the structure of social networks, we picked those that we believe better representing the structure of OPNs, but also able to provide some insights or patterns on their dynamics. The goal of this paper is *not* to propose new metrics for capturing the evolution of OPNs, but to reuse existing metrics in an evolving fashion in order to capture the dynamics. These metrics are presented hereafter.

4.1   Metrics Computed at the Personal/Ego Network Level

In this section we present a set of metrics with their respective definitions applied to undirected OPNs and that are computed at the personal network level.

Number of nodes and edges. The two metrics are defined in Definition 3. The OPN in Fig. 2-a has $n = 7$ and $m = 9$. We compute the number of nodes and edges to capture the OPN's size and to detect its change over time when nodes and edges are added and/or deleted.

Definition 3. *If $G'(V', E')$ is an OPN as defined in Definition 2, then $n = |V'|$ and $m = |E'|$ are, respectively, the number of nodes and the number of edges composing G'.*

Density. The density (or connectedness [12]) of a network, defined by Definition 4, assesses how much connected are the actors of the network.

Definition 4. *The density D of an undirected personal network $G'(V', E')$ is $D = 2 \times m / (n \times (n - 1))$, where m and n are the number of edges and of nodes of the network.*

For instance, the OPN in Fig. 2-a has $D = 0.42$. A high density means that the nodes are well connected; for instance, a complete graph (Fig. 3-a) has $D = 1$. On the contrary, a low density indicates a low number of edges between the OPN's nodes. Thus, the density of an evolving OPN describes the evolution of its connectedness (whether the density is increasing or decreasing).

Global clustering coefficient (Transitivity Index). The global clustering coefficient (GCC), introduced in [18] and defined in Definition 5 for OPNs, quantifies the transitivity in random graphs. The transitivity indicates that if a node x is connected to y and y is connected to z, then nodes x and z are likely to be connected. In a network, these structures are called *triangles* or *closed triplets*.

Definition 5. *The global clustering coefficient of $G'(V', E')$ (undirected personal network) is defined as $GCC = 3 \times T/C$, where T is the number of triangles in G' and C is the number of connected triples in G' (three nodes with at least 2 edges).*

The OPN in Fig. 2-a has 3 triangles and 22 connected triples, thus its $GCC = 0.409$. We want to compute GCC on OPNs to verify if (and how) the triangles characterize OPNs. Given a network, if $GCC = 1$, then every triad is a triangle (i.e. in complete OPNs, such as Fig. 3-a); if $GCC = 0$, then no triangle is present (i.e. in a star OPN, Fig. 3-b). The GCC was widely addressed in OSNs' evolution studies [7,14,17], as triangles were observed in many real OSNs and several OSNs' evolution models are based on them.

Average clustering coefficient (Average Watts-Strogatz Clustering Coefficient). This metric, introduced in [25] and defined in Definition 6, allows to characterize how much, in average, a network is locally clustered. The metric is computed by averaging the local clustering coefficients (defined later in Sect. 4.2) of the nodes.

Definition 6. *The average clustering coefficient ($< C >$) of an undirected personal network $G'(V', E')$ is $< C > = \sum_{x \in V'} C_x/n$, where C_x is the local clustering coefficient of node x, $\forall x \in V'$ and n is the number of nodes.*

$< C >$ ranges between zero and one. A value close to zero means that in average, the nodes are part of limited transitive relationships, while a value close to one indicates that the nodes participate in many transitive relationships (i.e. in complete OPNs, such as Fig. 3-a). For OPNs, we are interested in computing both clustering coefficients, GCC and $< C >$, to compare their evolution over time. Moreover, $< C >$ might provide a more precise idea of the connectivity of nodes in OPNs because it focuses on the local connectivity, meanwhile GCC is computing the connectivity over the whole network (which is counter intuitive in OPNs according to Definition 2).

Degree centrality and average degree centrality. The degree centrality of a node, introduced in [11] and defined in Definition 7, is the number of connections that the node has in the OPN.

Definition 7. *The degree centrality of node x (deg_x) in an undirected personal network $G'(V', E')$ is given by $deg_x = \sum_y e_{xy}$, where $e_{xy} = 1$ if an edge exists between the nodes x and $y \in V'$, and $e_{xy} = 0$ otherwise.*

For OPNs, we compute the degree centrality over all nodes for two purposes: (1) to check if the nodes' degree is following a power law distribution and (2) to compute the average degree ($< deg >$) of all the nodes in the OPN, defined below.

Definition 8. *The average degree $< deg >$ of an undirected personal network $G'(V', E')$ is given by $< deg >= \sum\limits_{x \in V'} deg_x/n = 2 \times m/n$.*

Power law distribution. The power law distribution of nodes' degrees is a property that appears in many real OSNs. For a network, it consists in having few nodes with a high degree and many nodes with low degree. Named the preferential attachment, it is the main property governing the majority of evolution models.

In order to verify if the nodes' degrees are following a power law distribution, we compute the degrees (as described in Definition 7) of all the nodes in the OPN. If verified, the degree distribution of the nodes should take the form $P(x) = cx^{-\alpha}$, where $P(x)$ denotes the fraction of nodes in the OPN having degree x, c is a normalization constant and α represents the exponent of the power law distribution function. If an OPN has a power law degree distribution, it means that the number of nodes with degree x is proportional to $x^{-\alpha}$ and α is the slope of the distribution and ranges typically around 2 or 3. When α is high, the number of nodes with high degree is smaller than the number of nodes with low degree. The personal network given in Fig. 2-a follows a power law distribution with $\alpha = 3.17$.

For OPNs, our aim is to check if the power law distribution holds, as in the case of OSNs. This information will allow us to validate whether the evolution models based on preferential attachment are suitable for OPNs and to what extend or not.

Ego's maximum degree of separation (k-max). In the Definition 2 of OPNs, the parameter k is used to limit the nodes part of the OPN, since only the alters that are at a maximum distance k from the ego can be part of the k-personal network of the ego. For a 2-personal networks, $k = 2$ and the alters are at a maximum distance of 2 from the ego. Note that by distance between two nodes, we mean the shortest path length between those nodes. By k-max, defined in Definition 9, we capture the maximum distance between the ego node and all alters reachable from the ego, and we observe how k-max changes when the OPN evolves. Moreover, we check if the 6-degree of separation principle

[22, 23], validated in real world OSNs [13, 15], is satisfied for OPNs. The 6-degree of separation, known as the "small world" phenomenon, suggests that each pair of nodes inside an OSN is connected via a shortest path of average length 6.

Definition 9. *The ego's e maximum degree of separation (k-max) in a undirected personal network $G'(V', E')$ is given by $k - max = \max_{x \in E'}(d(e, x))$, where $d(e, x)$ is the shortest path length between the ego node e and every node x reachable from e.*

4.2 Metrics Computed at the Ego Level

Ego degree centrality. In Definition 7, we presented the degree centrality of any node x in the OPN. We compute deg_e in order to capture how the number of ego's direct connections is evolving over time (in the OPN in Fig. 2-a, $deg_e = 6$). Below, we define the degree centrality of the ego node.

Definition 10. *The degree centrality deg of ego e in an undirected personal network $G'(V', E')$ is given by $deg_e = \sum_x e_{ex}$, where m_{ex} denotes that an edge exists between the ego node e and another node $x \in V'$.*

Betweenness centrality. The metric, introduced in [11] and defined in Definition 11, assesses the extent to which a node is between all the other nodes in the network. In [12], the betweenness centrality is introduced only for 1-personal networks, thus the Definition 11 was adapted to apply to k-personal networks. To this end, we do not restrict x and y to nodes directly connected to the ego, but x and y have to be at a maximum distance k from e. A high ego betweenness means that the ego participates in many shortest paths in its OPN (e.g. in the OPN in Fig. 2-a, $B_e = 0.76$) and reveals its importance inside its OPN (e.g. in the star personal network in Fig. 3-b the ego is the unique intermediate on all shortest paths between each pair of nodes and $B_e = 1$). When the OPN is evolving, we observe whether the importance of the ego is affected; thus more information about the structural changes in the network while evolving is revealed, e.g. if an ego's betweenness decreases, then OPN alters become more and more connected over time (thus ego becomes less important).

Definition 11. *The betweenness centrality of an ego e (B_e) inside its undirected personal network $G'(V', E')$ is $B_e = \sum\limits_{x \neq y \neq e} S_{x,y}(e)/S_{x,y}$ for every pair $(x, y), x, y \in V'$, where $S_{x,y}$ is the number of shortest paths between x and y in G', and $S_{x,y}(e)$ is the number of those passing through e.*

Local clustering coefficient (Watts-Strogatz clustering coefficient [25]). While the global clustering coefficient and the average clustering coefficient capture the transitivity inside a (personal) network, the local clustering is computed at a node level to detect the transitivity inside a node's immediate neighborhood (nodes directly connected to ego), as defined hereafter. For OPNs, we compute this metric only at the ego level (C_e) to capture the ego's connections at the 1st level. C_e ranges in the interval $[0, 1]$. A high local clustering coefficient indicates that most of ego's alters are connected with each other, while a low one indicates that only few links exist between ego's alters (e.g. in the star personal network in Fig. 3-b, $C_e = 0$). Thus, when the OPN evolves, by computing this metric, our aim is to observe the changes in the 1st level ego's alters connections rate which affects ego's importance.

Definition 12. *The local clustering coefficient of node x (C_x) in the undirected personal network $G'(V', E')$ is $C_x = 2 \times m_x / deg_x (deg_x - 1)$, where m_x is the number of edges between neighbors of x and deg_x is the degree of x.*

Effective size. This metric, introduced in [4] and defined in Definition 13, is computed for 1-personal networks and quantifies the connectedness of ego's 1-level alters. It is based on the notion of redundancy. A personal network of the ego e has redundancy if e's alters are connected with each other. In order to facilitate the effective size interpretation, we compute the efficiency (Eff). The efficiency norms the effective size of a personal network by the actual number of ego's alters deg_e as given hereafter $Eff = E/deg_e$. Compared to the effective size, the efficiency is easier to evaluate since it ranges in $[0, 1]$. A high effective size (and efficiency) reflects the fact that the redundancy is low i.e. the alters are not well connected with each other (e.g. in the star network in Fig. 3-b, $Eff = 1$). As for the local clustering coefficient, the effective size/efficiency allows us to capture the degree of connectedness between ego's alters and so the loss or gain of importance of the ego when the 1-personal network evolves over time.

Definition 13. *The effective size E of e in the undirected 1-personal network $G'(V', E')$ is $E = deg_e - Red$, where deg_e is the degree of e and Red is the redundancy defined as $Red = 2 \times m_e / deg_e$, where m_e represents the number of edges between e's alters.*

In this section, we presented the set of metrics that we will use in the analysis of the co-authorship OPNs' evolution. We provide in Table 2, as an example, the computation of all the above metrics on the OPN given in Fig. 2-a.

5   Online Personal Networks Evolution Study

5.1   Dataset Description

We have chosen to perform the analysis on OPNs from DBLP (Digital Bibliography & Library Project) Computer Networks dataset[1]. We constructed from DBLP the network of co-authorships with connections between pairs of authors who share at least one publication in the field of Computer Networks. The corresponding co-authorship network graph (undirected, since the relationship is symmetric) holds 13854 authors (nodes) and 32946 co-authorships (edges), and reflects those authors who have published in the period 1971–2013 and who do

---

[1] https://aminer.org/citation.

not belong to independent communities but belong to the giant component of the whole graph of scientific collaborations in Computer Networks area in 2013.

The evolution of a scientific collaboration network from time t to time $t + 1$ consists in the addition of new authors (nodes) that join the network and create new collaborations (edges) with existing authors that were in the network at time t. New edges can also appear between two authors already in the network at time t, as well as between two new authors joining the network at time $t + 1$. Since in our current analysis we do not exploit link weights, edges between existing nodes are not considered. In this context, the t parameter corresponds to the year in which a co-authorship was established (year of the published paper). Thus, one can capture the co-authorship network at a given starting time point and observe how this network evolves by the addition of nodes and edges until a final time point.

In our case, the aim is not to study the evolution of collaboration network as a whole, but to understand the evolution of the personal collaboration networks of a set of individual authors (egos) over time in an effort to understand if the evolution of the personal networks shares common characteristics, patterns or trends or if the behavior is specific to each personal network. To do so, we have split our data into 5 parts; each part is composed of a set of authors (egos) that have started publishing on a given year ($dataset_1$ holds authors that had their first publication in 2004, $dataset_2$ contains authors that had their first publication in 2005, and so on). In Table 3 we give in the third column the number of authors analysed per part, while the last column contains the time window on which we studied the evolution per part. We started studying the evolution of each part two years after the dataset's authors joined the network since we have observed that during the first two years a considerable fraction of personal networks remains unchanged (do not evolve in terms of nodes' and edges' addition), which is an interesting observation.

In the remainder of this section, we describe the methodology we used to analyze the DBLP data set, which relies on the metrics we presented in Sect. 4 focusing on understanding personal collaboration networks' evolution.

5.2   Description of the analysis

The analysis of the set of selected online personal networks is performed via the computation of the set of metrics described in the previous section over the different time-steps (each time-step corresponds to a year in our case). At the end we try to consolidate the observed behavior of the metrics over the personal networks and over the years in order to reach, wherever possible, a common conclusion.

To do that, we use PERSONA (PERSonal Online social Networks' Analytics) platform [6] in order to extract, from the entire network of collaborations, the desired personal network of a given ego, and then we compute all metrics on the extracted network. To extract a personal network, we need to specify the dataset of which the ego is part (e.g. $dataset_1$), the $year$ (possible values depending on the dataset presented in Table 3) and the k value (we distinguish five values for k, from 1 to 5). We stopped at 5 because, as it is observed in Fig. 1i and discussed thereafter, there are very few personal networks with $k - max$ values of 6 and 7 and no personal networks with $k - max$ between 8 and 13 and after 13 each personal network joins the giant component. Thus, for a given dataset and a specific metric, we will compute all the values of the metric for the authors (i.e. the ego/personal networks) for each *year* value and each k. For example, the density of dataset $dataset_1$, is computed as the value of the density for the personal network of each author inside $dataset_1$ on each year from 2006 to 2013 and for each $k = 1, 2 \ldots, 5$. For the case of the effective size, the local clustering coefficient and the degree centrality, we stop at $k = 1$ since these metrics are relevant only for 1-level personal networks.

Then, in order to assess the evolution of each metric through all the personal networks for the same dataset, we make two types of plots (for each couple $(year, k)$): (i) one of the value of the metric computed for each personal network; and (ii) one that represents the distribution of the values of the metric through all the personal networks in the same dataset. By using both types of plots, we can observe the tendency that a given metric has in terms of increasing or decreasing through the years and observe the behavior when k changes. In the next subsection, we provide the results of these representations and discuss the observed behavior of each metric.

5.3   Metrics Evolution Trends Detected via the Analysis

Before presenting the findings for each metric, we precise that the obtained results for all the metrics are the same for all the 5 datasets. Thus, in the following, we choose to report the results observed on $dataset_1$ which has the largest time window for studying the evolution.

Number of nodes and edges. In co-authorship networks nodes and edges are only added over time and cannot be removed. It was not possible to identify a single rate with which nodes and edges are added over the years. However, the role of edges in shaping the evolving structure of a personal network, will be further clarified as we discuss the rest of the metrics that follow.

Density. The density quantifies how well connected the nodes composing the personal networks are. When $k=1$, we observe a large proportion of personal networks with a density equal to 1 (see Fig. 1d) with density distribution on 2009 (we obtained the same distribution on the other years) which means that all the nodes are connected with each other at this level where personal networks are frequently composed of only few nodes (2, 3 or 4). This proportion decreases as the personal networks grow with nodes that are joining them but that do not necessarily connect to all the existing nodes. In 2013, some personal networks keep their density at 1, but in general the tendency is that the density decreases over the years. This tendency is also valid for $k = 2, 3, 4, 5$ where no personal network has a density equal to 1 and all of them get it decreasing to reach very low values at the last years (Fig. 1a).

The observed behavior is justified by the fact that generally when authors publish for the first time and join the network, they link to the set of authors with whom they share this first publication which explains at the beginning the emergence of complete networks at $k = 1$. Then, as years pass, if an author has new collaborations, they will not include necessarily all the previous collaborators of the author, and so the density decreases, and this regardless of the k. The behaviour is the same with the one reported in [1] for the whole collaboration network extracted from a collection of papers in High Energy Physics Theory.

Global clustering coefficient and average clustering coefficient. As presented in Sect. 4, we want to measure the transitivity inside co-authorship personal networks via two metrics: (1) the global clustering coefficient (transitivity index) and (2) the average Watts-Strogatz clustering coefficient. While the first one captures the global transitivity of the personal network and the second one expresses the transitivity around the nodes, we want to check if both metrics behave the same or not. In the literature, e.g. in [16], the authors claim that both metrics represent the clustered architecture of the network, with a small difference on value scaling. A more recent work [9] is discussing the divergence of these two metrics on a particular graph structure named *windmill graphs*.

Windmill graphs (an example is presented in Fig. 4) are characterized by the presence of a central node that is surrounded by cliques composed of nodes that are completely connected with each other and with the central node but that do not have any connections with the other cliques (or have few connections in real world networks where cliques are overlapping). We believe that such structure can arise in personal networks especially when coming from scientific collaboration networks as stated in [9], where the authors prove the presence of windmill graph structures inside both collaboration and citation networks. Moreover, they have showed the divergence of the two clustering metrics.

Thus, in our work, we aim to test if: for collaboration personal networks the two metrics behave in the same or different ways; if the change of the two metrics over time shows the same or inverse tendency; and if the windmill graphs appear as a case for the personal networks in any time during their evolution over time.

We will discuss the observed trend for each metric separately. As observed for the density, at $k = 1$ a high proportion of author's personal networks have a global clustering coefficient that is equal to 1 because personal networks at this level are usually complete. This proportion, as again observed for the density, is not present anymore for $k = 2$. We also distinguish at $k = 1$, a set of personal networks with a global clustering coefficient of 0 (Fig. 1c). This is due to the absence of triangles because we are in the case of a personal network with only two nodes and one edge connecting them. But, as the personal networks grow over time, triangle are formed and so, the global clustering of such personal networks will get a value different than 0. Concerning the trend over the years, the global clustering coefficient decreases which means that there is less transitivity caused by the fact that there are fewer connections among the alters regardless of k. These observations are consistent with the earlier discussion about the density.

For the average clustering coefficient, for $k = 1$ and in the early years, a significant set of personal networks hold the maximum average clustering coefficient value (equal to 1), because these personal networks are complete graphs. Similarly, we observed some personal networks with an average clustering coefficient equal to 0 due to the absence of triads around the nodes (see Fig. 1b). We notice that in general $\forall k = 1..5$, the value of the average clustering coefficient is high with a tendency of increasing through the years. The same tendency was observed for the whole collaboration networks in the Mathematics and Neural Sciences fields in [3].

Thus, when the personal networks are evolving over time , the global clustering coefficient and the average one exhibit opposite behaviors, since the first one gets decreasing and the second on gets increasing (see Fig. 1e). We can notice that, while the average clustering coefficient is high and gets higher with years, the global one gets lower and lower. This is compatible with the observations about windmill graphs in [9] where the authors claimed that this kind of graphs are locally clustered but globally poorly clustered, which is also verified for our personal networks.

The underlined observations are explained by the fact that in the personal networks of scientists, a publication will involve the creation of a clique between the authors of that publication where each one is connected to the other which explains the high average local clustering coefficient around nodes. But, the fact that a given author can over time have publications with new collaborators that will not in the most of cases concern the old ones, will from one side decrease the global clustering inside the personal network, and from the other side increase the average clustering coefficient. This could be explained by the fact that scientists during their career are led to change institutions and work places, collaborate with new authors (e.g. PhD students) and even change their research focus.

Power law distribution. In order to check the existence of a power law distribution over the degrees of nodes part of co-authorship personal networks, we have used the approach proposed in [5]. Thus, we provide as input a vector of discrete values representing the degrees of nodes of the personal network for which we want to perform the test, and we get as output the answer of the test (*true* if the personal network follows a power law distribution, *false* if not) depending on the $significance$ parameter computed by the algorithm, and the estimated parameter α of the power law distribution function. For the evolution, the power law distribution means that when new nodes arrive to the personal network, they will tend to connect to nodes having a high degree, which will lead to the appearance of some highly connected nodes in the personal networks and many weakly connected nodes.

Computing the Power Law for personal networks of $k = 1, 2, 3$ was not possible because the networks were too small and the computation did not make any sense. Figures 1f and g represent, for $k = 4$ and 5 respectively during the period

2006–2013, the proportion of personal networks that follows (in blue) or not (in red) a power law distribution for their degrees. The Power Law holds for $k = 4$, while the true/false proportion remains about the same over the years. At $k = 5$, the results are not so conclusive and the tendency is inverted since 2010 when the proportion of personal networks having the power law test to false over-passes true. This later observation is interesting since we expected that, larger personal networks as it is the case when $k = 5$, to confirm the properties that were observed for global networks as the power law distribution of networks' nodes degrees as proved in [3] for the case of scientific collaboration networks.

We also observed that the proportion of personal networks that returned false was increasing with k (for $k = 4$ and $k = 5$) and over the years. We were unable to verify the main reason why this happens and this behavior is the opposite than the expected one. One possible but still unverified explanation could be that the evolution of personal networks connects previously existing cliques (see the clique between the 15 nodes labeled from 1589 to 1603 in the example Fig. 5). In a clique, each node is highly connected locally so the merging of two cliques into one creates a new, bigger and more connected clique; thus we have more nodes with higher degrees and subsequently the Power Law tests fail for all these nodes. This behavior is compatible with what happens in many cases in co-authorship networks, where we frequently see collaborations among groups and a new publication has as authors all (or almost all) the members of both groups. As we already stated, unfortunately, it was not possible to verify this explanation experimentally. However, if we consider the co-authors network as a whole, the degrees' distribution follows a power law (as observed in [3]); this comes from the fact that at a large scale the proportion of such highly connected authors becomes negligible compared to the majority of authors that have a small amount of collaborations.

Ego's maximum degree of separation (k-max). As presented in Sect. 4, we would like to know the maximum shortest path from the ego observed in a personal network. We performed the computation of $k - max$ on our dataset for each ego and for each year from 2006 to 2013. The plot in Fig. 1i gives the distribution of $k - max$ value over all the years. We distinguish two phases: (1) the first around $k - max = 4$ to 7 with very few personal networks having such values, and (2) the second one ranges from $k - max = 13$ to 25. We notice that no personal network has a $k - max$ value between 8 and 12, whatever the year.

The evolution of $k - max$ over the years reveals that after reaching a certain size, the number of nodes composing the personal network will remain stable while $k - max$ can vary (the maximum $k - max$ achieved equals 25). This size corresponds to the whole network giant component size for each year (Fig. 1j). The fact that no $k - max$ value is between 8 and 12 is due to the interconnection among existing personal networks which makes jump $k - max$ from 7 to a value ≥ 13. As we report in Table 1, the average $k - max$ computed for each year from 2006 to 2013 ranges between 15 and 19 approximately, which means that it is constantly higher than 6. We conclude that the "6-degrees of separation" property that characterizes "small world" networks does not hold in our case and thus the collaboration network we are studying does not represent a "small world" network. On the contrary, in [8] is found that the 6-degrees of separation phenomenon is valid when they studied the collaboration network of scientists who publish in the Database area.

Table 1. Average $k - max$ per year.

Year	2006	2007	2008	2009	2010	2011	2012	2013
Average $k - max$	18.18	18.39	18.00	16.61	17.82	16.18	15.82	15.81

Ego degree centrality and personal networks average degree. After computing the degree centrality over personal networks's nodes to check the existence of a power law distribution, we now present the results obtained for both: the degrees of egos and the average degree for all personal network's nodes. Firstly, for the degree of the egos of our dataset, we observed that in general only few egos are very highly connected while most of them have low degrees (Fig. 1h). The distribution remains almost the same even when years pass. Secondly, for the average degree over all the nodes composing the personal networks, we would like to check if the assumption of a constant average degree, made by existing full networks evolution models, is valid when considering personal networks instead of full networks. We found that for $k = 1$, when the personal network is created, the average degree remains low (there are a lot of values around 1 and 2) even when the personal network grows. Then, from $k = 2$ we have seen that there are fewer values around 1 and 2 and the average degree increases to concentrate around a value of 4 or 5 (see Fig. 1k).

Our results are consistent with what was found in [3] when studying the whole network of scientific collaboration in both Mathematics and Neural Sciences fields (in both networks the average degree increases over time); even if it is not the common behavior observed in real world social networks as addressed above. The average degree increase over time is explained by the fact that when a new publication is registered, its authors form necessarily a clique (all coauthors of the same publication are connected with each other); then when another publication comes with mainly the same authors and some new ones, these new ones are added to the clique. This results in increasing the average degree among the alters of a personal network while maintaining the same k for the personal network.

Betweenness centrality. We evaluate the ego betweenness centrality over time in order to observe how its importance is affected when the personal network is evolving. For $k = 1$, we observed that a significant number of egos have a betweenness of 1 in their personal networks, which reflects the case of star networks where the ego is the unique intermediate between its alters. Then for $k = 2$, this trend is not present anymore, as more nodes are included in the personal networks. We also observed, that many egos have a betweenness of 0 regardless of k, which denotes that no shortest path between any pair of nodes is passing through the ego. In this situation the ego is considered as not important since its alters can reach each other without passing through it. This is an important conclusion for the information diffusion in personal networks because it shows that many times the personal network evolves without the active participation of the initiating node and that the ego node does not influence significantly after a point in time the other members of the network.

The ego betweenness evolution over time was observed as increasing for $k = 2$ and $k = 3$ and decreasing for $k = 4$ and $k = 5$. We explain the fact that it increases for $k = 2$ and $k = 3$ by the addition of nodes that connect to ego's alters but, in order for these new nodes to reach the other alters of the ego, they have to go by the ego and thus ego's importance is increasing. In the context of scientific collaborations, this situation is emerging when, for example, one of ego's co-authors makes a new collaboration with a new set of authors. Then, the path between one of the new collaborators and an old ego co-authors includes necessarily the ego. For $k = 4$ or 5 we were unable to verify the reason of the different behaviour. One plausible explanation is that since (as discussed earlier) cliques have already started forming then in this case of personal networks, new collaborations happen between cliques in a more complete way (two groups collaborating) and thus the evolved network contains a new bigger clique. Having local cliques decreases the importance of the ego. Another plausible explanation could be that the ego is not getting new connections (collaborations) as the ego in the network in Fig. 6, or are making few ones, where one (or more) of his alters (co-authors) are leading the main dynamics inside its personal network (as the alter "383" inside the circle). Unfortunately, it was not possible to verify either one of these explanations experimentally.

Local clustering coefficient and efficiency. We grouped the local clustering coefficient and efficiency results discussion because both metrics are computed at the ego level and concern only 1-personal networks ($k = 1$). We have observed that both the local clustering coefficient and the efficiency decrease over the years, when new nodes integrate the 1-personal networks. This indicates that ego's alters are less connected with each other over time; and it means that new collaborations for 1-level personal networks happen mainly with the ego and usually do not involve many of the other existing collaborators. This explains also the fact that the average clustering coefficient in a 1-level personal network is increasing; the new connections are usually "complete" either with the ego or with the ego and few of the existing collaborators so we have all the possible triangles materialized (the local clustering coefficient of the alters equals 1 which increases the average clustering coefficient of the 1-personal network). One the other hand, for the ego this means that he has a lot of incomplete triangles since the new nodes will not participate in materializing the majority of the possible triangles with the rest of the alters.

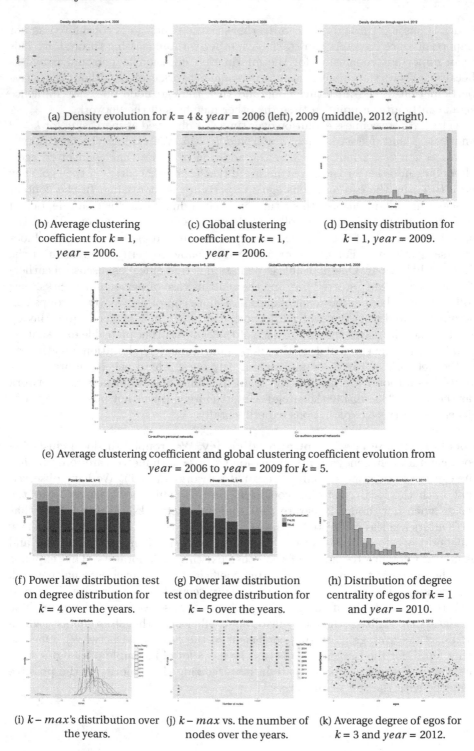

(a) Density evolution for $k = 4$ & $year = 2006$ (left), 2009 (middle), 2012 (right).

(b) Average clustering coefficient for $k = 1$, $year = 2006$.

(c) Global clustering coefficient for $k = 1$, $year = 2006$.

(d) Density distribution for $k = 1$, $year = 2009$.

(e) Average clustering coefficient and global clustering coefficient evolution from $year = 2006$ to $year = 2009$ for $k = 5$.

(f) Power law distribution test on degree distribution for $k = 4$ over the years.

(g) Power law distribution test on degree distribution for $k = 5$ over the years.

(h) Distribution of degree centrality of egos for $k = 1$ and $year = 2010$.

(i) $k - max$'s distribution over the years.

(j) $k - max$ vs. the number of nodes over the years.

(k) Average degree of egos for $k = 3$ and $year = 2012$.

Fig. 1. Evolution of personal network metrics. (Color figure online)

Table 2. Metrics computation example.

Metric	Value
k	1
Number of nodes	7
Number of edges	9
Density	0.42
Number of triangles	3
Number of connected triples	22
Global clustering coefficient	0.409
Average clustering coefficient	0.695
Power law test	True with $\alpha =3.17$
Ego degree	6
Ego betweenness	0.76
Average degree	2.57
Local clustering coefficient	0.2
Efficiency	0.83

Table 3. The description of the different parts of the used DBLP data set.

Dataset	Year of first appearence	Number of analysed authors	Time window
1	2004	560	2006 to 2013
2	2005	594	2007 to 2013
3	2006	1096	2008 to 2013
4	2007	1029	2009 to 2013
5	2008	1256	2010 to 2013

(a) 1-personal network. (b) 2-personal network.

Fig. 2. Personal networks examples.

(a) Complete personal network. (b) Star personal network.

Fig. 3. Particular personal networks examples.

6 Influence of Metrics' Trends on Personal Networks Evolution

In Table 4, we summarize the main observations that we made in the previous section regarding the evolution of the metrics in the co-authorship personal networks. We report in the second column the observations regarding the parameter

Table 4. Summary of the observations of metrics' evolution.

Metric	Observations regarding k	Observations over years
Ego Degree Centrality (deg_e) (only for $k = 1$)	few egos with a high degree, low degree (2 or 3) frequent	OPN keeps the same tendency while evolving
Local Clustering Coefficient (C_e) (only for $k = 1$)	many networks have $C_e = 1$ some have $C_e = 0$	decreasess
Efficiency (only for $k = 1$)	-	decreases
Density (D)	$\forall k \in \{1, 2\}$, D is high	$\forall k$, decreases
Global Clustering Coefficient (GCC)	$k = 1$, high GCC	$\forall k$, decreases
Average Clustering Coefficient ($< C >$)	$\forall k$, high $< C >$	$\forall k$, increases
Number of nodes and edges	-	$\forall k$, both increase
Average Degree	for $k = 1$, around 1, 2 for $k \geq 2$, around 4, 5	$\forall k \in \{2, 3, 4, 5\}$, increases
Ego Betweenness Centrality (B_e)	$k = 1$, for many networks $B_e = 1$ $\forall k$, for many networks $B_e = 0$	$\forall k \in \{2, 3\}$, increases $\forall k \in \{4, 5\}$, decreases
Power law distribution	$\forall k \in \{1, 2\}$, verified $\forall k \in \{3, 4, 5\}$, less verified	$\forall k \in \{1, 2\}, \forall year$, verified in more than 80% of cases $\forall k \in \{3, 4\}$, less verified especially for $year \geq 2011$ for $k = 5, \forall year \geq 2011$, not verified
$K - max$	-	$\forall year \geq 2011$, $k - max > 13$ for all the personal networks

k, while in the third column we present the observed evolution trends for each metric over the different time steps (years).

In the following subsections, we firstly discuss the insights from the metrics about the evolution of co-authors personal networks for the special case when $k = 1$ and then we discuss the more general case of $k > 1$.

6.1   Observations for the Evolution of 1-Personal Networks

From our observations, 1-personal networks constitute a particular case. Indeed, a large proportion of 1-level personal networks are small star networks with few nodes characterized with an ego betweenness centrality of $B_e = 1$ along with a weak ego degree (for example, if an ego has 2 connections, these two connections

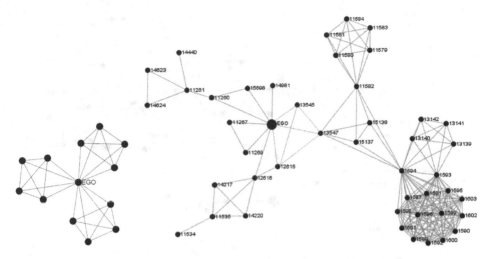

Fig. 4.   Windmill
graph $W = (3, 4)$.

Fig. 5. Example of a clique formation.

correspond to two independent collaborations, the ego in this case plays a key role given its important position). Furthermore, in other cases we observe the exact opposite phenomenon: because of the co-authorship network's specificity where when we have many coauthors in a paper, these coauthors are connected in a complete subgraph, a considerable set of 1-personal networks is consisting of complete graphs, characterized with an ego betweenness of $B_e = 0$.

For both the egos' degrees and egos' betweenness, when the network evolves over time, the situation remains the same. More precisely, the evolution affects mostly the connections among alters who were characterized at the beginning with an important number of connections and then they become less connected over time as new alters join the 1-level personal network (the density, the local clustering and the efficiency decrease). However the addition also of nodes (alters) keeps the average degree for the 1-level personal network nodes low.

6.2   Observations for the Evolution of Personal Networks with $k > 1$

The personal networks with $k = 2, 3, 4, 5$ are characterized by both a decreasing density and global clustering coefficient. The nodes joining the personal network create very few edges compared to the possible number of edges that can be created among the nodes, and thus we get a lower density and a lower transitivity at the personal network level. At the local level, the average clustering coefficient was observed to be high and gets higher when the personal networks are growing which indicates a high local clustering around the nodes, not necessarily the ego anymore. We can explain that by the fact that co-authorships are made generally between 3, 4 or 5 authors and the emergence of a new collaboration imply the

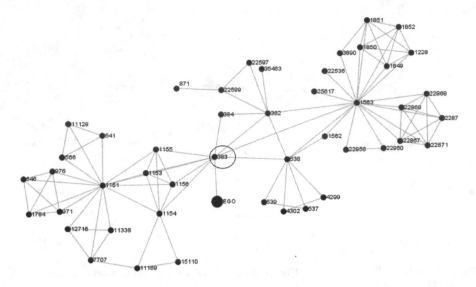

Fig. 6. Personal network ($k = 4$) example for low ego betweenness extracted from co-authorship networks.

creation of a highly clustered local structure since all the authors that made this collaboration are going to be already connected with each other.

The trends we discussed so far concerns all personal networks with k from 2 to 5. Nevertheless, ego's betweenness centrality behaves differently: it was increasing for $k = 2, 3$ but decreases for $k = 4, 5$. On the one side, the increase at $k = 2, 3$ is due to the addition of nodes around the ego that form disconnected groups of alters (as the windmill graph example) and the ego plays the role of a linker between them. On the other side, when we consider a $k = 4$ or 5, then as we already discussed, existing cliques might merge into bigger and more connected cliques and thus the ego's betweeness decreases. This hypothesis was not validated experimentally yet, though. Additionally, the power law distribution of degrees is better satisfied when $k = 4$ than $k = 5$. This hypothesis has not been verified experimentally yet.

6.3   Towards Developing Evolution Models for OPNs Using the Observations of Metrics' Evolution

The aim of this paper is not only the understanding of how OPNs change over time, but also to discover properties that one can benefit from in order to provide an evolution model dedicated to OPNs. From the results summarized previously in this section, we ended up with some insights on how personal networks' structure changes over time as nodes and edges are added. We discuss here the following type of evolution: at time t, an OPN has n_t nodes and m_t links; at times $t + 1$ we need to predict both the number of new nodes entering the network and how these nodes connect to the personal network (and also, if any, the new links created).

Firstly, an evolution model should be able to describe 1-personal network's connections, that include ego-alter and alter-alter connections. We discovered that, at $k = 1$, nodes are not very connected and maintain, in average, a low degree over time; also, the main dynamics takes place for the connections among alters since, as nodes are integrating the personal network at this level, alters become less and less connected (density, local clustering and efficiency decrease). So the evolution model should assign over time fewer edges between alters.

Secondly, it is important to note that, when a personal network evolves, if at time t, the maximum distance from the ego (in terms of shortest path length) is equal to k, then at time $t + 1$, it may be equal to $k + i$ (and not $k + 1$), as new nodes connect to existing nodes that are at k distance from the ego. This is following our definition of an OPN, as presented in Sect. 2. The evolution of a given metric over time might be different depending on k as it is the case for the betweenness centrality. Indeed, at the second and third levels ($k = 2, 3$), given that the connections' number among alters decreases (decreasing density), ego importance gets higher (increasing betweenness for $k = 2, 3$). Then, as the personal network grows, nodes get farther from the ego ($k > 3$), and ego's importance falls over time (decreasing betweenness for $k = 4, 5$) since new shortest paths are emerging between alters that do not include the ego. So, the potential model needs to account for the transition phase when the ego node moves from a key position in its personal network to a less important one. As discussed earlier our unverified explanation discusses the possibility that the personal network will get higher degree nodes and structures of cliques (which increases the average degree of the personal network) as time goes by. This is consistent with the behaviour of the average local clustering coefficient, which increases for the same personal networks, indicating stronger local connections.

Finally, an evolution model for personal networks needs to know at which moment the personal network joins the entire network (the giant component). With the computation of $k - max$, we have seen that we can keep evolving the network and exceed $k = 6$ which is the distance suggested as separating any two nodes inside a social network (6° of separation). We confirmed experimentally that the average shortest path in our personal networks between any ego and any node of its personal network fluctuates on average between 15 and 19 for all time steps (years) and that the personal network will join the giant component when $k - max$ reaches 13. This is a very useful observation since it tells us that after a specific number of time steps personal networks are able to reach all the nodes in the online social network. From an information diffusion perspective, this allows us to disseminate information to everybody after remaining for some time active in a social network.

7   Conclusions and Future Work

In this paper, we performed an analytical study of personal networks of coauthors in scientific publications, with the goal to use the results of this study to understand the evolution of the corresponding personal networks. We selected a set of metrics that characterizes the personal networks' structure and that allowed us to capture the change over time of this structure. We were interested to understand not only the specific values of the metrics but mainly how these values change over time.

However, some elements of this understanding remain incomplete and need to be investigated more deeply. These include, for example, the quantification of the presence of some specific structures (as windmills, cliques) in order to characterise precisely personal networks structure and attribute correctly the reason for some of the observed behaviour. In our future work we plan to accomplish that via the use of clustering methods depending on the metrics we studied and their evolution over time that will hopefully verify the now suspected evolution patterns. In this way, we will be able to establish accurately the effect that has each of these specific structures in the evolution of personal networks. Then, effective models can be provided for describing personal networks dynamics.

References

1. Amblard, F., Casteigts, A., Flocchini, P., Quattrociocchi, W., Santoro, N.: On the temporal analysis of scientific network evolution. In: 2011 International Conference on Computational Aspects of Social Networks (CASoN), pp. 169–174. IEEE (2011)
2. Arnaboldi, V., Conti, M., Passarella, A., Dunbar, R.: Dynamics of personal social relationships in online social networks: a study on twitter. In: Proceedings of the First ACM Conference on Online Social Networks, pp. 15–26. ACM (2013)
3. Barabâsi, A.-L., Jeong, H., Néda, Z., Ravasz, E., Schubert, A., Vicsek, T.: Evolution of the social network of scientific collaborations. Physica A **311**(3), 590–614 (2002)
4. Burt, R.S.: Le capital social, les trous structuraux et l'entrepreneur. Revue française de sociologie, pp. 599–628 (1995)
5. Clauset, A., Shalizi, C.R., Newman, M.E.J.: Power-law distributions in empirical data. SIAM Rev. **51**(4), 661–703 (2009)
6. Djemili, S., Marinica, C., Malek, M., Kotzinos, D.: A definitions' framework for personal/egocentric online social networks. In: 7éme conférence sur les modéles et l'analyse des réseaux: Approches mathématiques et informatiques (MARAMI'16) (2016)
7. Ebel, H., Davidsen, J., Bornholdt, S.: Dynamics of social networks. Complexity **8**(2), 24–27 (2002)
8. Elmacioglu, E., Lee, D.: On six degrees of separation in dblp-db and more. ACM SIGMOD Rec. **34**(2), 33–40 (2005)
9. Estrada, E.: When local and global clustering of networks diverge. Linear Algebra Appl. **488**, 249–263 (2016)
10. Fisher, D.: Using egocentric networks to understand communication. IEEE Internet Comput. **9**(5), 20–28 (2005)

11. Freeman, L.C.: Centrality in social networks conceptual clarification. Soc. Netw. **1**(3), 215–239 (1978)
12. Freeman, L.C.: Centered graphs and the structure of ego networks. Math. Soc. Sci. **3**(3), 291–304 (1982)
13. Goel, S., Muhamad, R., Watts, D.: Social search in small-world experiments. In: Proceedings of the 18th International Conference on World Wide Web, pp. 701–710. ACM (2009)
14. Holme, P., Saramäki, J.: Temporal networks. Phys. Rep. **519**(3), 97–125 (2012)
15. Lattanzi, S., Panconesi, A., Sivakumar, D.: Milgram-routing in social networks. In: Proceedings of the 20th International Conference on World Wide Web, pp. 725–734. ACM (2011)
16. Li, M., O'Riordan, C.: The effect of clustering coefficient and node degree on the robustness of cooperation. In: 2013 IEEE Congress on Evolutionary Computation (CEC), pp. 2833–2839. IEEE (2013)
17. Moriano, P., Finke, J.: On the formation of structure in growing networks. J. Stat. Mech. Theory Exp. **2013**(06), P06010 (2013)
18. Newman, M.E.J.: The structure and function of complex networks. SIAM Rev. **45**(2), 167–256 (2003)
19. O'malley, A.J., Arbesman, S., Steiger, D.M., Fowler, J.H., Christakis, N.A.: Egocentric social network structure, health, and pro-social behaviors in a national panel study of americans. PLoS ONE **7**(5), e36250 (2012)
20. Sarmento, R., Cordeiro, M., Gama, J.: Visualization of evolving large scale ego-networks. In: Proceedings of the 30th Annual ACM Symposium on Applied Computing, pp. 960–962. ACM (2015)
21. Sutcliffe, A., Dunbar, R., Binder, J., Arrow, H.: Relationships and the social brain: integrating psychological and evolutionary perspectives. Br. J. Psychol. **103**(2), 149–168 (2012)
22. Travers, J., Milgram, S.: The small world problem. Phychology Today **1**, 61–67 (1967)
23. Travers, J., Milgram, S.: An experimental study of the small world problem. Sociometry **32**, 425–443 (1969)
24. Viswanath, B., Mislove, A., Cha, M., Gummadi, K.P.: On the evolution of user interaction in facebook. In: Proceedings of the 2nd ACM Workshop on Online Social Networks, pp. 37–42. ACM (2009)
25. Watts, D.J., Strogatz, S.H.: Collective dynamics of small-world'networks. Nature **393**(6684), 440–442 (1998)
26. Yanhong, W., Pitipornvivat, N., Zhao, J., Yang, S., Huang, G., Huamin, Q.: egoslider: visual analysis of egocentric network evolution. IEEE Trans. Vis. Comput. Graph. **22**(1), 260–269 (2016)
27. Zhao, J., Glueck, M., Chevalier, F., Wu, Y., Khan, A.: Egocentric analysis of dynamic networks with egolines. In: Proceedings of the 2016 CHI Conference on Human Factors in Computing Systems, pp. 5003–5014. ACM (2016)

Author Index

Printed in the United States
By Bookmasters